PRAISE FOR THE AUTHOR

"If you're concerned that bullshit communications may be plaguing your organization and its decision processes, you should be. If you're concerned there is nothing to do to identify and dispose of this insidious social substance, don't be. Kevin Duncan's book is the concise and pointed answer that any serious business leader or decision maker should have at their bedside."
John V. Petrocelli, Professor of Psychology, Wake Forest University, TedX presenter, *Why Bullshit is More Dangerous Than a Lie*, author, *The Life-Changing Science of Detecting Bullshit*

"The world is currently drowning in bullshit, so any book that helps us cut through it is most welcome."
Dave Trott, Author, *The Power of Ignorance*, *Creative Blindness and How to Cure It*, *Creative Mischief*, *Predatory Thinking* and *One Plus One Equals Three*

"A brisk, lucid exploration of a subject that so often prompts only a shrug of bemusement. It's an antidote to the fakery, pretentiousness and obfuscation that mar so much of today's political and professional discourse."
Henry Hitchings, Author, *The Language Wars: A History of Proper English*

"Clear thinking needs clear talking. Kevin makes the link. Razor sharp, witty and incisive."
Max McKeown, Author, *#Now*

Thanks to those who charmingly took the trouble to reply to my requests for endorsement, declining in a bullshit-free way. I appreciate it. Daniel Levitin, Giles Coren, Gyles Brandreth, Jeffrey Pfeffer, Jeremy Paxman, Quentin Letts, Tim Harford.

Published by
LID Publishing
An imprint of Lid Business Media Ltd
The Record Hall, Studio 304,
16-16a Baldwins Gardens,
London EC1N 7RJ, UK

info@lidpublishing.com
www.lidpublishing.com

A member of:

BPR⊛
businesspublishersroundtable.com

© Kevin Duncan, 2022
© LID Business Media Limited, 2022

Printed in Latvia by Jelgavas Tipogrāfija

ISBN: 978-1-911671-50-3
ISBN: 978-1-911671-51-0 (ebook)

Cover and page design: Caroline Li

THE BULLSHIT-FREE BOOK

HOW TO COMMUNICATE CLEARLY AND RECLAIM OUR LANGUAGE

KEVIN DUNCAN

MADRID | MEXICO CITY | LONDON
NEW YORK | BUENOS AIRES
BOGOTA | SHANGHAI | NEW DELHI

FOR OTHER TITLES
IN THE SERIES...

CONCISE
ADVICE
LAB

SMALL BOOKS: BIG IDEAS

CLEVER CONTENT, DYNAMIC IDEAS, PRACTICAL
SOLUTIONS AND ENGAGING VISUALS –
A CATALYST TO INSPIRE NEW WAYS OF THINKING
AND PROBLEM-SOLVING IN A COMPLEX WORLD

conciseadvicelab.com

CONTENTS

PART THREE: WHAT TO DO ABOUT IT: A BULLSHIT NAVIGATION GUIDE

PREFACE

In many respects, the title of this book is a complete lie. It's not remotely bullshit-free. In fact, it's full of the stuff, but that's the only way to understand it properly — by analyzing it and working out how things should really be expressed.

I had a lot of fun researching the 100 examples offered here. A brief look at the history of bullshit shows that people have been talking rubbish since speech was invented, but one definition in particular caught my eye.

Soldiers use the term 'bulling' to refer to a polishing technique that gives leather products an extremely high shine. This form of cleaning has no practical application other than to present an image of exemplary cleanliness. The process is intended to 'bullshit' the inspector of cleaned items, such as boots, into believing that the job has been done properly.

The finished effect leaves the surface of the leather highly reflective. The irony is that the oils in the polish never actually reach the leather, so that the slightest touch to the laminated layers of brittle polish can crack or even shatter it like glass.

It looks great, but it's flawed.

It's the same with bullshit. It can sound great, but it's flawed.

For a full compendium of 2,000 bullshit phrases, read this alongside its sister volume, *The Business Bullshit Book*.

Let's eradicate this stuff from our language if we possibly can.

Kevin Duncan
Westminster, 2021

"A great many people think they are thinking when they are merely rearranging their prejudices."
– William James

PART ONE

LIFE IN A WORLD OF BULLSHIT

I. **INTRODUCTION**

Writing a book about bullshit is a fairly strange thing to do. In fact, few have ever done it. There are one or two books, a few articles, and some dictionaries. But detailed analysis of what it is and why people use it is pretty much impossible to find.

On the surface, it's a hilarious subject, full of ludicrous phrases and an endless supply of nonsense that we can all enjoy, usually at someone else's expense. Look again, and it becomes apparent that it can be a lot more dangerous than people think.

Bullshit is the vocabulary that provides the scaffolding for spin, fake news and what has in some circles even come to be known as 'post truth'. Despite the fact that we are now surrounded by the stuff, several vital questions about the topic remain unanswered or, at best, thinly investigated.

If we are to deal with bullshit effectively, or even just cope with it, there are certain things we really need to understand. We will see that not all bullshit is necessarily a bad thing. It might be annoying and tiresome but could still serve a purpose if it enables effective communication. That's a big if, but it is possible. Understanding how dangerous it can be is essential for all businesses and people in their jobs. If you can see it for what it is, then you are less likely to be hoodwinked or misled.

HOW DO WE KNOW IF SOMETHING IS BULLSHIT?

In Part Two we will examine 100 different examples of bullshit, working out where they come from, and whether they serve any kind of communication purpose. In each, a better, plain English alternative will be suggested. We can see immediately that this is subjective, so there are bound to be plenty of readers who scan the examples and say: *"Hang on, that's not bullshit!"* Here are some vital factors to consider.

CONTEXT IS EVERYTHING

The words and phrases someone chooses to use can be bullshit in one context and not in another. If a jet pilot or aeronautical engineer talks about pushing the envelope, then it may well be legitimate. If a marketing person does, then it's probably not. It is also essential to work out who is talking. Does the person saying the phrase have integrity? Do they know what they are talking about? If the answer is no to either of these, then we are almost certainly in the presence of a bullshitter.

EFFECTIVE COMMUNICATION IS EVERYTHING

If a bullshit word or phrase just about communicates what it intends to, then it's relatively harmless, if somewhat annoying. So if your boss says they want to touch base, they are guilty of mild bullshit but at least you know that they want a meeting on that topic. If it doesn't communicate effectively then it is either a pure lie or some degree of bullshit. So if your boss talks about leaning in, squaring the circle, opening the kimono or walking the walk going forward, then you may have difficulty understanding what they are talking about. That's where bullshit fails, assuming that the person using it actually wants to be correctly understood. Of course, they may not, and we will look at that phenomenon later.

EVERYTHING IS OPEN TO MISINTERPRETATION

Everything is open to (mis)interpretation. Plain, clear language has the least chance of being misunderstood. Bullshit has the most. So anyone using bullshit needs to consider whether they want to be understood or not. This is where we will delve into the more insidious uses of bullshit – when it is *deliberately* intended to confuse or obfuscate. This is where 'normal' people would do well to get inside the mind of the bullshitter. Unless you know why they do what they do, you will be ill-equipped to deal with the fallout of their bullshit.

OVERUSE AND FATIGUE

Overuse and fatigue of many words explains why they lose their meaning and effectiveness. As with most fads, a word might become popular and to begin with it may have greater effect through novelty. It may then enter a plateau of sameness, and eventually lose its power through overuse. Overuse can still mean effective communication, albeit not distinctive communication. Companies and executives who choose to use cliché, bullshit and overused words and phrases therefore do so to their own detriment, even if they don't realize it. This can effectively mean a failure to communicate due to their audience being overexposed to such world-weary vocabulary and them zoning out as a result.

CULTURAL UNDERSTANDING

(Lack of) cultural understanding is another factor in failure to communicate. Using jargon, cliché, acronyms, in-the-know words and phrases can be acceptable if done in the right company. A group of specialized engineers are entitled to a language of their own when talking to their own kind. However, the moment the specialist steps out to address a wider lay audience, all the rules change. Failing to understand an audience will lead to inappropriate choice of words and phraseology and so deplete the speaker's ability to get across what they have in mind.

THE PURPOSE OF THIS BOOK

So, the whole thing is a messy business. Whether it is context, misinterpretation, lack of understanding or a mischievous desire to confuse everybody, we all need to understand what's going on a great deal better. This book hopes to be humorous but informative. Simply pointing out that 100 words or phrases are bullshit doesn't get the reader very far, albeit there is some amusement along the way. Much more important is to understand what on earth is going on so that you can navigate intelligently through an awkward situation or the hard-to-understand demands of a bullshit-ridden boss. Anyone is, of course, welcome to *disagree* that the examples in the book are bullshit, but such a view comes with a health warning: should anyone specifically choose to use these words, without understanding their origin and true meaning, then they only have themselves to blame.

II. A BRIEF HISTORY OF BULLSHIT

According to Henry Hitchings, author of *The Language Wars*,[1] language evolves all the time. People have always debated the state of English, from Chaucer through Dickens and Shakespeare to the modern day. People get angry about it, arguing about slang, abbreviations, buzzwords (itself a buzzword?), vocabulary imported from other languages, and even the abuse of apostrophes. His message is that we need to engage with language more – thinking and talking about it in a more effective way. It's the same with bullshit, which is just another type of language, albeit a mangled one.

POLITICS AND THE ENGLISH LANGUAGE

'Politics and the English Language' is the title of a superb essay written by George Orwell in 1945.[2] Although published 75 years ago, it could have been written yesterday and the points would be valid. All you have to do is substitute the word bullshit for 'language' in Orwell's essay and you have a consummate summary of what is wrong with much modern speech. He asserted that political chaos is connected with the decay of language, and vice versa – we can probably bring about some improvement by starting at the verbal end.

In other words, lousy thinking leads to rubbish expression, but it also works the other way round. Poor expression causes lazy thinking, too. Language and thought are interrelated. The language becomes ugly and inaccurate because our thoughts are foolish, and lazy language makes it easier for us to have foolish thoughts. If thought corrupts language, language can also corrupt thought. That, in a nutshell, is the invidious power of bullshit.

THE PREVALENCE OF HUMBUG

Fast forward 40 years and another eminent thinker was chipping in on the subject. Philosopher Max Black wrote an essay in 1983 called 'The Prevalence of Humbug.' At this stage the word bullshit had not yet appeared in the literature – it was regarded as too crude. (It had, however, appeared on film. There were several uses of the word in 1976's *All The President's Men*). Black called it 'humbug,' was worried that it was on the rise, and offered some thoughts on what you can do about it. This is the first moment when we find a genuine attempt to define what bullshit really is. He identified first- and second-degree humbug.

FIRST-DEGREE HUMBUG is deceptive misrepresentation, short of lying – especially by pretentious word or deed – of somebody's own thoughts, feelings or attitudes.

SECOND-DEGREE HUMBUG is when the speaker is self-deluded. In other words, they really do believe what they are saying, although to everyone else it's complete bollocks.

He also distinguished between the speaker's *message* and his or her *stance*. The message is what is explicitly or implicitly said about the topic in question. The stance is their beliefs, attitudes and evaluations. So, both the words and the context can define whether we are in the presence of a bullshitter.

III. WHAT IS BULLSHIT?

Black identified a range of other words for humbug including (my modern definitions added):[3]

BALDERDASH: senseless, stupid, exaggerated talk
CLAPTRAP: absurd or nonsensical talk or ideas
RUBBISH: very bad, worthless, useless (words or ideas)
CLICHÉ: a phrase or opinion that is overused and lacks original thought; platitude
HOKUM: trite, sentimental or unrealistic
DRIVEL: nonsense, originally referring to saliva or mucus flowing from the mouth or nose
BUNCOMBE: that's Buncombe County in North Carolina, from a remark made by its congressman in 1838, who defended an irrelevant speech by claiming that he was 'speaking to Buncombe'
GIBBERISH: unintelligible or meaningless speech or writing
TAUTOLOGY: a phrase or expression in which the same thing is said twice, in different words
IMPOSTURE: pretending to be someone else in order to deceive others
QUACKERY: dishonest claims to have specialist knowledge
NONSENSE: all the above – literally, 'not sense'

We could just as easily add twaddle, tommy rot, waffle, hot air, baloney, cobblers, codswallop, blarney, guff and hundreds of other words and expressions.

Eminent Princeton University professor Harry G. Frankfurt develops the theme.[4] Constituent elements of bullshit are *misrepresentation of somebody's own thoughts, feelings or attitudes.* He compares bullshit to shoddy goods — produced in a careless or self-indulgent manner, and never finely crafted.

Frankfurt believes that the essence of bullshit is:

* A lack of concern with the truth
* An indifference to how things really are
* A kind of bluff

BULLSHIT IS NOT JUST VERBAL

In their book, *Calling Bullshit*, Carl Bergstrom and Jevin West suggest that we are surrounded by bullshit, in many forms: "Politicians are unconstrained by facts. Science is conducted by press release. Start-up culture elevates hype to high art. The world is awash with bullshit and we are drowning in it."[5] The reason is that everyone is trying to sell you something, and there is no limit to it because our complex language allows us to produce it in infinite variety:

"Bullshit involves language, statistical figures, data graphics and other forms of presentation intended to persuade or impress an audience by distracting, overwhelming, or intimidating them with a blatant disregard for the truth, logical coherence, or what information is actually being conveyed."[5]

Now we can see that as time has gone on, bullshit has seeped into pretty much every area of life and morphed from the written or spoken word into other media, such as data and graphics. This wider definition of bullshit covers a lot more than just words — it's any form of misrepresentation, intended or otherwise.

LIES OR TRUTH

As we try to hone in on a definition of bullshit, we can see that the job gets harder and harder. The word is an all-encompassing term for a multitude of sins. The biggest mistake people can make is to view bullshit as simply lies. It's not that simple. It might be, but it might not. It is far more helpful to view bullshit as working along a spectrum of lies to truth, taking pit stops at a slight untruth at one end and slight overclaim at the other, with a swirl of obfuscation in between.

BULLSHIT

Right-minded people often find this thought completely baffling. It's often easy to spot when someone is lying, but that isn't what bullshit is. The bullshitter has no regard for lies or truth — they just grab the nearest thing to get them out of the immediate situation they find themselves in. That is why it is so bewildering for many.

EMPTY WORDS AND LAZINESS

This is where we need some detective work concerning the person speaking. Are they chucking these words around intentionally, to mislead, or unintentionally, due to ignorance or just plain laziness? It's a crucial distinction, and something that is even harder to work out if you do not know the person in question, or perhaps the context in which the words were said.

For the moment, let's take devious politicians and company executives out of the equation, suspend disbelief and assume that most people who use bullshit are not necessarily evil-minded. If that's the case, the majority of bullshit you hear is probably people of many different types lazily throwing phrases and words around, without much thought, but nevertheless without malice. These are words and phrases empty of meaning and appropriated incorrectly. This material is without question aggravating, but it is relatively harmless and can be useful as a shortcut for fast communication. Even better if the speaker knows where these expressions come from and then uses them appropriately, but that may be too much to ask of most bullshitters.

BULL OR NOT BULL?

Looking at the matter in a broad, practical way, consider these thoughts about bullshit:

- *It's not bullshit* if it accurately sums up what you have in mind, and the people you're speaking to understand it and act accordingly
- *It is bullshit* if you use a phrase and don't know where it comes from or what it actually means
- *It's probably bullshit* if you use a combination of linguistic laziness and ignorance about where phrases come from or what words really mean
- *It might be bullshit,* but it might not, depending on who says the words and the context in which they are spoken
- *A bullshit-free version* of a statement can also be bullshit, if it's a lie or any form of overclaim
- *Sometimes you just can't tell*; As philosopher G. A. Cohen said: "Bullshit is unclarifiable unclarity."[5]

THE GREAT CAVEAT: IF IT'S TRUE

And finally, everything in this book is subject to what I call the great caveat: *If it's true*. This is a caveat that can be applied to anything and everything. If it's not true, it's a lie. If it is true, then it's not technically bullshit, but it can still be expressed in a bullshit way. It's all the rest in the middle that we have to watch.

IV. WHY PEOPLE DO IT

THE SLIDING SCALE

We have established that there is an unholy mess of bullshit between lies at one end of the spectrum and truth at the other. Now, let's look at why people resort to bullshit. On an approximate sliding scale — from mild and relatively harmless to strong and dangerous — there are seven main reasons why people bullshit.

1. TO IMPRESS

Talking insincerely is often used to impress. It is being misleading without necessarily lying, deliberately leading you to draw the wrong conclusion by saying things that are not technically *un*true. Sophisticated bullshitters have an ability to put themselves in the place of the person they want to bullshit, and imagine what impression will be created by what type of bull. These people think that if they use more complicated words, jargon and so on, you will think they are more impressive.

2. TO PERSUADE

Bullshit can be persuasive or evasive. Persuasive bullshit aims to win an argument or convey a point of view that people end up agreeing with. In this respect, remember that the bullshitter is neither on the side of the truth nor the side of what's false. They don't care whether the things they say describe reality correctly. They just pick any snippet of information, or make things up, to suit their purpose.

3. TO COVER UP

The philosopher and academic Harry G. Frankfurt said that the production of bullshit is stimulated whenever someone's obligations or opportunities to speak about a topic exceed their knowledge of the facts that are relevant to the topic.[4] When that's the case, the bullshitter is involved in a cover-up job. It might be to conceal something that has been done badly, or perhaps not even done at all. But in most cases it will be used to prevent you from realizing that they really don't know what they're talking about.

4. TO EVADE

Evasion is a classic bullshit approach. In essence, the bullshitter doesn't want to confront the issue or discuss the topic, either because they are too lazy or they don't want to face the consequences. So, they become evasive, using bullshit as a smokescreen or deflection technique to distract the listener from the main point. Remember that valuing truth is of no central interest to them.

5. TO CONFUSE

Chess Grandmaster Garry Kasparov said, "The point of modern propaganda isn't only to misinform or push an agenda. It is to exhaust your critical thinking, to annihilate the truth."[6] Creating confusion and doubt is a great way of doing this, and often enables the bullshitter to get off the hook or get out of a tight situation. Does the bullshitter lie? Not necessarily. They are phony rather than false. The bullshitter is faking things, but this doesn't necessarily mean that they get things wrong. As such, they have much more freedom than someone who tells the truth or lies, because they require no anchor point for what they are saying. Confusion plays to their advantage.

6. TO MANIPULATE

According to Thomas Erikson, author of *Surrounded By Psychopaths*,[7] the main driving forces behind why people manipulate each other are:

- **THEORETICAL:** wanting to learn more. This is harmless unless they use the information deviously
- **PRACTICAL-ECONOMIC:** to gain possessions and money. This is devious and may also be illegal
- **AESTHETIC:** to be stylish or acquire stylish trappings. This is vanity
- **SOCIAL:** to look better in front of others. More vanity, usually showing off
- **INDIVIDUALISTIC:** to gain personal power. This gets closer to dangerous
- **TRADITIONAL:** to gain standing in hierarchies, such as a religious group

Bullshit facilitates all these manipulative desires.

7. TO MISLEAD

American comedian George Carlin once quipped: "Honesty may be the best policy, but it's important to remember that apparently, by elimination, dishonesty is the second-best policy."[8] Here we reach the closest bullshit gets to becoming a lie. Many use it deliberately, to mislead. By twisting words and phrases, the speaker stops just short of lying by creating a blur of misleading wordsmithery that bamboozles the listener into thinking that things are fine, or that it was nothing to do with the person speaking.

v. **HOW DANGEROUS IS IT?**

THE IMPORTANCE OF LANGUAGE

Language in the workplace matters – it can inspire or deflate, so senior people need to choose their words carefully. Those working in large organizations need to balance their annoyance at this type of language with a means of working with it, because it won't go away, and the constant protestor could come across as a cynic. The language we speak affects the way we view the world and works through two perspectives: language as a mirror can reflect views, but language as a lens can bring them into focus.

BAD LANGUAGE = BAD THINKING

There has been a huge debate about whether language *reflects* the character of its speakers, or *influences* their thought processes. Does the language we speak affect the way we view the world? Guy Deutscher, author of *Through The Language Glass*, believes the answer is yes. Orwell certainly believed it, too. So, if we follow that logic, lazy language such as bullshit is extremely dangerous because it fosters poor thinking.

THE PROBLEM OF SAMENESS

There may be no immediate danger from everyone using a lot of bullshit until we encounter the problem of sameness – that is, thousands of empty words trying to be distinctive or trying to suggest that a company or product is different from, or better than, the others. This is a whole genre of bullshit claiming, or wanting to claim, that an organization or product is more original, pioneering, innovative, unique, inventive, or distinctive than their competitors. In this respect, bullshit is mostly failing as a communication device.

DEVALUING TRUTH

James Ball, author of *Post-Truth: How Bullshit Conquered The World*, takes it a step further. He reckons that the rise of a political, media and online infrastructure has hugely devalued truth.[9] Bullshit is so powerful that it can get you into the White House or remove a country from Europe. Everybody is spreading it: politicians, old media, new media, fake media, social media and probably you, whether you realize it or not. Most depressingly, we often fall for it because it satisfies our basic need for stories, sensationalism and a desire to confirm our own beliefs. It is also extremely profitable for those who peddle it, so there is a commercial imperative too.

THE EFFECT ON LEADERSHIP AND CULTURE

The bullshit that surrounds the subject of leadership inhibits people from fulfilling their potential and excludes potential leaders from believing that they, too, could lead. That's the view of Chris Hirst, in his book *No Bullshit Leadership*.[10] In other words, bullshit even has the power to inhibit your career. Certain careers involve more bullshit than others. According to Frankfurt, "The realms of advertising and of public relations, and the nowadays closely related realm of politics, are replete with instances of bullshit so unmitigated that they can serve among the most indisputable and classic paradigms of the concept." It's ubiquitous, he says. "One of the most salient features of our culture is that there is so much bullshit. Everyone knows this."

THE PRICE OF CLEANING UP

Bergstrom & West believe that it is essential that people realize "that:

1. *bullshit takes less work to create than to clean up,*
2. *takes less intelligence to create than to clean up,*
3. *spreads faster than efforts to clean it up."* [5]

They note that a number of eminent observers illustrate these points well:

"An idiot can create more bullshit than you could ever hope to refute."
Uriel Fanelli[5]

"The amount of energy needed to refute bullshit is an order of magnitude bigger than that needed to produce it." Alberto Brandolini[5]

"Falsehood flies, and truth comes limping after it." Jonathan Swift[5]

"A lie will gallop halfway round the world before truth has the time to pull its breeches on." Cordell Hull[5]

WATCH YOURSELF

And finally, American author Neil Postman warns us against ourselves: "At any given time, the chief source of bullshit with which you have to contend is yourself."[5] Most of us are now familiar with filter bubbles — online communities that act as an echo chamber, so that we only ever reinforce views that we already hold. This may have been less harmful when we simply bought a newspaper to reflect our own views. But in a digital world, this bullshit is often the only view of the world that we see. Now that's truly dangerous.

BULLSHIT RATING SYSTEM

 : Should be banned outright

 : Downright dangerous

 : Potentially harmful

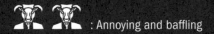 : Annoying and baffling

: Annoying but harmless

PART TWO

CONTEXTS

INTERNAL
BULLSHIT

Looking inside companies first, we move broadly from the macro settings of vision and values statements, large-scale meetings and all-staff presentations, down to the micro face-to-face interactions with bosses and colleagues.

1.
VISION
AND VALUES

Arguably one of the worst contexts for bullshit ever devised. As the mania for having a vision and values has gripped businesses, the proliferation of bullshit has been almost unstoppable.

Vision and values provide the breeding ground for scores of flabby adjectives that are rarely true, usually including a healthy dollop of authenticity, passion and of course the ubiquitous *world class*, which is never true and is impossible to prove, except perhaps in competitive sport.

1.1: ALWAYS IN BETA

> *"We're always in beta. We never stop trying to improve. Like sharks, we keep swimming. The sun never sets at Super Corporation."*

ORIGIN:

This phrase comes from the world of technology. A trial 'beta' release allows testers to work out the bugs in software before the product goes on general release. This admirable idea has spawned a copycat phenomenon in other businesses, many of which have nothing to do with software. Claiming to be 'always in beta' is effectively announcing that the product or company is still being tested or is always in need of improvement.

USE & ABUSE:

To the uninitiated, this phrase may mean nothing at all. On the plus side, a product or company that is continually trying to improve should be applauded, so long as the claim is true. On the minus side, an unfinished product could simply remain that way, and as such be permanently subpar. In many markets, a company or product that is always in beta should be treated with deep suspicion.

BULLSHIT-FREE VERSION:

Constantly improving.

> *"Let's accept that nothing is ever perfect and keep trying to make things better."*

BULLSHIT RATING:

1.2: **AUTHENTIC**

> "Come on guys, we need to be authentic around this!"

ORIGIN:

This concept originated in philosophy. In existentialism, authenticity is the degree to which a person's actions are congruent with their beliefs, regardless of external pressure. In business, the main question is whether a company does what it claims it does or has the genuine proof to back up their projected image.

USE & ABUSE:

Of course, some companies have excellent origins, and still hold true to their founding principles. That's a good thing. Others, however, make up huge fabrications to suggest that they are authentic when they are not. Classic deceptions include brands that suggest that their recipes have been around for centuries, when they were actually only drummed up a couple of years ago. Such claims also fall into a classic trap: it is not really a company's job to claim to be authentic — it is up to their customers to deduce that from the way the company behaves. Being authentic is good; seeking authenticity as an end in itself is not.

BULLSHIT-FREE VERSION:
Genuine.

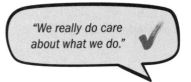

> "We really do care about what we do." ✓

BULLSHIT RATING:

*Interestingly, Stanford University business theorist Jeffrey Pfeffer believes that authenticity is misunderstood, overrated and may actually be impossible. Most leaders need to be inauthentic, subsuming their personal feelings and adjusting their behaviour to suit a variety of situations.[11]

1.3: **PASSIONATE**

> *"Here at Blowhard Corporation,
> we're super passionate about everything we do."*

ORIGIN:

Passionate is a word with several possible meanings. At its core, it means having strong emotion, sometimes of an uncontrollable nature. It is frequently associated with lust, desire and sexual matters. It has even been used in a religious context, to describe the suffering and death of Jesus. All in all, a mixed bag of meanings.

USE & ABUSE:

There is nothing wrong at a basic level with someone being passionate about what they do. In fact, it is probably desirable for job satisfaction. The abuse comes when (a) it's not true and (b) the subject matter is patently not something people would ordinarily get passionate about, as in, "We are deeply passionate about ball bearings." This is another example of the self-analysis trap: it is not a company's or a person's job to claim that they are passionate; it is up to their customers and colleagues to deduce it from their actions.

BULLSHIT-FREE VERSION:
Enthusiastic.

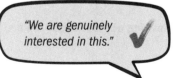

> *"We are genuinely
> interested in this."*

BULLSHIT RATING:

1.4: **PURPOSE**

> *"We have been working hard to work out the 'why' of what we do — our purpose, so to speak."*

ORIGIN:

Purpose used to be a perfectly normal word meaning the reason why something is done, or a person's sense of resolve or determination. This has now spawned an entire industry in which it appears that no company can do anything unless it has one. It seems that it is no longer sufficient simply to make things and sell them, or to provide a service in a straightforward manner, without a fuss.

USE & ABUSE:

Having a sense of purpose is important for the sanity of individuals and the quality of their work, and it may also help if a company has one. However, the outbreak of meaningless Venn diagrams full of worthy words doesn't necessarily improve the morale of a workforce or the quality of what a company delivers. Too much waffle about purpose remains just that: a collection of platitudes based on hot air and left somewhere on a meeting room wall after the all-staff presentation.

BULLSHIT-FREE VERSION:
Knowing why we do what we do.

> *"The reason why we do what we do is 'x'."*

BULLSHIT RATING:

1.5: WORLD CLASS

> *"Our products are truly world class."*

ORIGIN:

World class strictly means in the upper echelons of the best of its kind in the world. It is a truly mighty claim. The phrase originated in the arena of sport, when nations and individuals began to compete in tournaments such as the Olympic Games and the World Cup.

USE & ABUSE:

There is nothing wrong with aspiring to be the best, or truly excellent, but this phrase collapses in the absence of any satisfactory metric by which to measure such a claim. If a sportsperson or team beats every other contender in the world, then they are indeed world class. There is no equivalent whatsoever in the business or political world, leading to thousands of vacuous claims that can never be verified. Given that this phrase is never provable, it utterly lacks humility and is therefore a champion of bullshit.

BULLSHIT-FREE VERSION:

The best in the world.*

*If true.

> *"We believe we are the best, and here's the evidence."*

BULLSHIT RATING:

2.
BOARD
MEETINGS

In theory, board meetings should be orderly affairs, conducted by grown-ups using clear language and making intelligent decisions. In practice, anyone who has been in one knows that this is patently not the case, and the frequent failure of entire corporations proves the point about dysfunction at the top.

These meetings are often a hotbed of jealousy, mistrust, egotism and obfuscation. Even worse, the board member who wishes to seem impressive, while strangely picking up no action points or accountability, simply needs to deploy ample quantities of bullshit to get away with it, safe in the knowledge that their fellow directors are most likely doing the same.

2.1: **BENCHMARKING**

> *"We are benchmarking our capabilities against the best in the industry."*

ORIGIN:

Disputed. One theory suggests that the word comes from the positioning notch made by marksmen when guns were first mounted on benches for stability and more accurate aiming. Another claims that the term benchmark, or bench mark, came from the chiselled horizontal marks made by surveyors in stone structures that enabled them to insert steel spikes to support a bench for levelling rods.

USE & ABUSE:

Having a good working knowledge of the standards needed to succeed in a business category can be helpful, and looking at the qualities of a successful competitor could certainly encourage a poor-quality company to improve what it does. On the downside, benchmarking has two large flaws: 1) A tendency to make companies paranoid, spending most of the year worrying about and analyzing the competition instead of doing proper work; 2) A catalyst to make all companies in a category exactly the same, encouraging mediocrity and a lack of distinction.

BULLSHIT-FREE VERSION:
Comparing.

> *"We have compared ourselves with the competition and this is how we fared."*

BULLSHIT RATING:

2.2: GRASP THE NETTLE

"We need to grasp the nettle on this issue."

ORIGIN:
Pretty straightforward. The phrase has been around since 1884, and is based on the innate assumption that picking up a stinging nettle is going to hurt. So, it has become a euphemism for enacting a task that will almost certainly have unpleasant implications. Interestingly, it excludes the 'stinging' descriptor, which is probably a disservice to some other nettles, which can be grasped painlessly.

USE & ABUSE:
On the one hand, we all understand what this means, so the analogy communicates well enough: to summon up the courage to deal with a difficult problem. The context, however, often borders on the macho, as in: "We need to grasp the nettle on Project Peanut, Roger." Those using the phrase frequently take on something of a sadistic quality, either suggesting that doing something nasty will be fun, or just delighting in the fact that someone else will have to do the dirty deed.

BULLSHIT-FREE VERSION:
Tough action.

"We need to stop dithering and make this difficult decision."

BULLSHIT RATING:

OPEN THE KIMONO

> *"We want to get into bed with this potential purchaser, so we need to open the kimono."*

ORIGIN:

This is a blatantly sexist, and possibly racist, phrase that means to reveal the inner workings of a company or project in order to secure investment or sell the whole company. It probably stems from the rash of Japanese acquisitions of US companies in the '80s, especially in software. The sexual metaphor suggests revealing enough flesh before consummating the deal.

USE & ABUSE:

There are no circumstances in which this phrase is acceptable. We can be sure that it was not coined by a woman, and the American/Japanese male/female axis makes it racist as well as sexist. And in case you thought that this might be an age-old anachronism, as recently as 2012 the head of a major financial institution described his company as an 'open kimono' organization. Shocking stuff.

BULLSHIT-FREE VERSION:
Show the inner workings.

> *"We need to reveal how our company really works to show our potential partner."*

BULLSHIT RATING:

2.4: THINK OUTSIDE THE BOX

> "We desperately need new ideas, Janine. Get your team to think outside the box for once, will you?"

ORIGIN:

This phrase comes from the nine-dot matrix (or 'Gottschaldt figurine'), which challenges the solver to join all nine dots with four lines without removing the pen from the paper. The brain perceives the dots as a box, but the puzzle can only be solved by drawing the lines outside the apparent box. In other words, unless you 'think outside the box' you can't solve the problem. There is also a theory that the box in question is an advertising hoarding and that the ad industry adopted the phrase in the 1990s.

USE & ABUSE:

Used incessantly in modern business meetings to encourage people to be more inventive — a perfectly admirable request at base level. Sadly, it is an extremely lazy exhortation, which gives the listener no guidance whatsoever about what direction their thinking should take. The world's best problem solvers welcome, indeed demand, the freedom of a tight brief. In other words, tell me the constraints and I will work at the very boundaries of them to create something better.

BULLSHIT-FREE VERSION:

Come up with an inspired but feasible idea.

> "What ideas have you got that are different to what we've done before?" ✔

BULLSHIT RATING:

2.5: **WIN-WIN**

> *"This is a win-win situation, Dave."*

ORIGIN:
This phrase was coined by Victor Baranco, one of the founders of Lafayette Morehouse, a utopian community in California, in the '60s. But his definition of it involved *both* parties getting *everything* they want, creating good news all round. The modern interpretation of it is more a summary of compromise in which both sides lose something — almost lose-lose, in fact.

USE & ABUSE:
This one is a bit of a shocker, and is habitual fodder for macho salesmen everywhere, as catnip is to cats. If the principle behind it truly is that both parties have what they want, then that's a good thing. More commonly, though, it is a lazy substitute for, "For fuck's sake, squeeze some value out of this because the other lot have the upper hand." In its worst form, this phrase has morphed into win-win-win, which sounds both greedy and mathematically impossible.

BULLSHIT-FREE VERSION:
Both sides are happy.

> *"We need everyone to be happy with this agreement."*

BULLSHIT RATING:

3.
FINANCE
MEETINGS

These meetings are often populated by grey men and women in even greyer suits. Spreadsheets rule, as people earnestly hunch over forests of numbers or sit earnestly staring at impenetrable slides on the wall.

Much ruminating usually follows, but there's a game going on. Someone will chip in with an abstruse comment about ballpark figures, fiscal juggling and low-hanging fruit. Everyone nods sagely.

And then, someone spots a decimal point out of place in one cell of the 400th spreadsheet. All hell breaks loose, and the bullshit starts all over again.

3.1: **BALLPARK FIGURES**

> *"Just give me a ballpark figure."*

ORIGIN:

This phrase comes from the world of sport. Before official statistics were counted, a commentator would estimate the size of the crowd by looking around the stadium. It is named after a ballpark because it started in American baseball. A ballpark figure is a rough numerical estimate or approximation of the value of something that is otherwise unknown. Commonly used by finance or project management to estimate future results or the likely cost of projects.

USE & ABUSE:

There is nothing particularly wrong with asking for a rough estimate, but many people get confused about the parameters. Many have been fooled into providing what they thought was an estimate, only to find that a colleague, or indeed the whole budget submitted to the business, has turned that estimate into a fixed figure now taken as gospel. Targets are a particular culprit here, which is why they are so often missed. Since that can lead to a person being fired, always try to give a range rather than a single figure.

BULLSHIT-FREE VERSION:

Give me a range of likely cost.

> *"Give me a rough idea of how much this will cost."*

BULLSHIT RATING:

3.2: FUTUREPROOFING

> *"This will futureproof our business."*

ORIGIN:

You can futureproof something (a verb) or you can make it futureproof (an adjective), but nobody is sure whether to put a hyphen between the future and the proof. Futureproofing, in plain English, is the process of anticipating the future and developing methods to minimize the effects of shocks or stresses from future events. It probably comes from the world of industrial design or the medical and electronics industries.

USE & ABUSE:

As a communication device, the word just about succeeds. Protecting a company against (usually unwanted) future developments is admirable, but, really, who can accurately predict them? In almost every field, so-called experts are proven time and again to be wrong. So, in the wrong hands, this is merely a self-deluding notion that forthcoming events can indeed be predicted accurately, but it may be no more helpful than soothsaying, crystal ball gazing, navel gazing, pure guesswork, or placing your finger in the air and whistling Dixie.

BULLSHIT-FREE VERSION:

Our best shot at predicting what will happen next.

> *"All the information we have suggests that this will successfully guard against possible events in the future."*

BULLSHIT RATING:

3.3: **LOW-HANGING FRUIT**

> *"Right, team, let's go for the low-hanging fruit."*

ORIGIN:

'Fruit low hung' or 'fruit hanging low' have been part of the English language since at least the 17th century. However, the precise term low-hanging fruit was probably first used in an article in *The Guardian* newspaper in 1968. It refers to the easiest and simplest thing to do in order to achieve success or benefit in some way (sometimes called a quick fix).

USE & ABUSE:

Most people get the analogy that if the fruit (the desired prize) is hanging low, it will be easier to pick. As such, effective communication is achieved. However, the context in which it is used is frequently one of expedience: do the easy stuff first and see if you can get away with it; avoid hard work at all costs; take the path of least resistance; cut corners; exploit a situation to your advantage. It is also worth noting that fruit that hangs too low will simply rot on the ground.

BULLSHIT-FREE VERSION:

The easiest, simplest thing.

> *"Take the quickest route to get the job done."*

BULLSHIT RATING:

3.4: MASSAGE THE NUMBERS

> "I think we need to massage the numbers for the board here, Roland."

ORIGIN:
A true hybrid, with no clear origin. Massage is manipulation of human tissue by rubbing, kneading or tapping, and massaging the numbers is rearranging financial data or statistics to create a different conclusion.

USE & ABUSE:
Those not in the know might assume that a number is a number, but those who've witnessed how corporate finance departments really work may beg to differ. It boils down to a moral stance and a view on the extent of the massaging. Some might argue that a small tweak or percentage change won't hurt much, but others point to deceptive, often downright illegal, alteration of financial reporting to generate an entirely different picture, usually a favourable one. Related euphemisms include sleight of hand, legerdemain and malfeasance. Extreme cases have led to company closure or personal imprisonment.

BULLSHIT-FREE VERSION:
Misreporting the finances.

> "Change these numbers so they look more favourable."*

BULLSHIT RATING:

*Be aware that this could be an illegal instruction.

3.5: PUSH THE NEEDLE

> "We really need to push the needle on this one, guys!"

ORIGIN:

There are two possible sources for this. Old analogue recording equipment had VU (volume unit) meters that registered if enough signal was running through the device. If the signal was very weak, the needle wouldn't move at all. Cars have speedometers — the faster you go, the more you 'push the needle'.

USE & ABUSE:

The recording analogy seems a reasonable enough way to suggest squeezing out more effort. The automotive version is far worse, laced as it is with heavy macho overtones. This full-throttle, balls-to-the-wall, cock-of-the-rock expression has everything that testosterone-fuelled Sales Directors require, conjuring up images of fighter pilots, racing cars, speed and power — a veritable classic for pumping up the troops.

BULLSHIT-FREE VERSION:

Work as hard as we can.

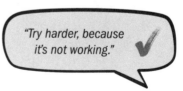

> "Try harder, because it's not working."

BULLSHIT RATING:

4.
ALL-STAFF PRESENTATIONS

All-staff presentations are frequently well intentioned, but they can descend into chaos. Sometimes what is being announced is simply not popular — a round of redundancies, for example.

On other occasions, troublemakers start asking the management awkward questions, and there is dissension in the ranks. The degree of insubordination is usually in direct proportion to how secretive or deceptive management have been.

Is the all-company meeting, or so-called 'town hall,' a genuine exchange of opinion or a smokescreen that tells you the information will be cascaded down, but that there is no silver bullet and failure is not an option? Read on.

4.1: **CASCADE**

> *"We need to cascade this information down to the troops, Emma."*

ORIGIN:

A cascade is a waterfall, and the word has been in use in French and Italian at least since the 1600s. It is both a noun and a verb, and has numerous applications in all sorts of fields, including biochemistry and electricity. In a modern context, it has entered the realm of bullshit by being used to explain the process of disseminating information in companies.

USE & ABUSE:

To cascade information in a company relies on the principles of hierarchy and gravity. People at the top decide something, and then want the news to fall like water down each status level until every member of staff gets the message. The desire for thorough communication is admirable, but it's not as simple as that. There are two main flaws: 1) If senior people were any good at communicating their intentions, they should do it themselves; 2) By disseminating important information through so many levels, they unwittingly set in train a whispering chain, in which the message inevitably becomes distorted.

BULLSHIT-FREE VERSION:
Make sure everyone knows.

BULLSHIT RATING:

> *"Inform all staff clearly, in one announcement."*

4.2: **FAILURE IS NOT AN OPTION**

> *"Project Binbag must succeed. Failure is not an option."*

ORIGIN:

This phrase is usually attributed to American Aerospace engineer Gene Kranz in connection with the Apollo 13 mission, but he never actually said it. In fact, it was coined by the scriptwriters of the *Apollo 13* film in 1995. It has since become much-loved by dictatorial business leaders wishing to put the fear of God into their employees.

USE & ABUSE:

The most positive thing one can say about this phrase is that, in the right hands, it could just about be a motivational exhortation to achieve an admirable goal. But it is fundamentally flawed for two huge reasons. First, it is not possible to have 100% control over whether you succeed or fail. Second, failure is not something you can choose, so there is no option in the first place. Consummate rubbish invented by Hollywood dramatists in order to sell a film.

BULLSHIT-FREE VERSION:
Make every effort to succeed.

> *"Do your very best and let's get on with it."* ✔

BULLSHIT RATING:

4.3: **GAIN TRACTION**

> *"We urgently need to gain traction on this, guys."*

ORIGIN:

Traction is the action of drawing or pulling something over a surface, especially a road or track. More precisely, it is the grip of a tyre on a road or a wheel on a rail. Its use was first recorded in 1605. That's the engineering view of it, but in medical circles it describes the process of gently pulling the neck or spine to relieve pressure. In its modern use in business, traction refers to the support or momentum needed to advance something or make it a success.

USE & ABUSE:

This phrase is the cause of significant confusion. There are half a dozen definitions of traction that precede today's common business use, and they are much more scientific and precise. But, when business people use it, that's not what they really mean. They are talking about momentum, speed and progress, which physical traction could actually slow down. All of which suggests that people in business probably have a pretty shallow understanding of physics.

BULLSHIT-FREE VERSION:
Enduring success.

> *"Let's make this a long-term success, not a short-term victory."*

BULLSHIT RATING:

4.4: **NO SILVER BULLET**

> *"There is no silver bullet here, Adrian."*

ORIGIN:

In folklore, a bullet made from silver was the only thing capable of killing a werewolf or witch. References date back hundreds of years and feature in tales by the Brothers Grimm, for example. Turing Award winner Fred Brooks used it as the title of a 1987 paper explaining that advances in software engineering would not be as fast as those in hardware development.

USE & ABUSE:

The phrase essentially means that there is no single answer that will guarantee a result, so, why not just say that? The majority of the time, there is a sense of desperation attached to it, which can be interpreted as: "This is too difficult for us to do." Leaders need to be aware that when they use it there are many possible interpretations, including the implication that this will be really difficult, take a long time, be really expensive, or even that it may never get done.

BULLSHIT-FREE VERSION:

Very difficult to solve.

> *"There is no single answer that will guarantee a result."*

BULLSHIT RATING:

4.5: **PIVOT**

> *"We had to pivot our business model to attract the investment we needed."*

ORIGIN:

As a noun, a pivot is a central point, such as a pin or spike, on which a mechanism turns. As a verb, it means to spin or turn around and face the other way, often at speed. First recorded in French in the 1300s, it was popularized in the US to describe the manner in which basketball players keep one foot anchored on the ground whilst rotating the body.

USE & ABUSE:

The uses above are legitimate, but the word is now sorely abused in modern business, both as a noun and verb. We pivoted the business. We had to pivot. Our pivot strategy took the market by storm. In this context, it's a deceptive and misleading word that throws up a smokescreen for its true meaning: that our original strategy was utterly useless, so we had to enact a complete change of direction.

BULLSHIT-FREE VERSION:

Head the other way.

> *"Our original strategy didn't work, so we're changing direction."*

BULLSHIT RATING:

5.
BOSSES

Bosses attract criticism like a lightning conductor, usually due to their disgraceful treatment of subordinates. So many of them demand immediate action on certain issues, whilst deflecting and obfuscating on others.

Once you've been told to get your ducks in a row, stick to your swim lane, take it offline and circle back by the end of play, you could indeed be forgiven for not knowing what the hell you are doing.

5.1: **CIRCLE BACK**

> *"I'll circle back to you on that next week."*

ORIGIN:

In surveys conducted by this author, this is one of the most consistently hated phrases used in business. It has a bewildering array of meanings, including to discuss it later, to report back after finding out more, and to return to a point in the same conversation or meeting. Its origin is unclear but is probably no more complex than coming back to the same place, having gone around in circles.

USE & ABUSE:

At face value, there's not much wrong with suggesting that you will return to a point once you're better informed, but the reason this phrase is so disliked is that it conceals a more deceptive intention. The prevailing view from subordinates is that bosses use it to deflect and avoid dealing with tricky topics, as in: "I'll circle back to you on your appraisal next week, Victoria."

BULLSHIT-FREE VERSION:

Respond when I am better informed.

> *"I don't know enough about this, so I'll get back to you when I do, as fast as I can."*

BULLSHIT RATING:

5.2: **DUCKS IN A ROW**

> *"We need to get our ducks in a row on this one, team."*

ORIGIN:

Date of origin: around the mid-20th century. Ducklings tend to follow their parents in a single-file line, whether on land or water, and this has become a metaphor for organizing tasks and schedules so as to be ready for the next step. Other sources suggest that the phrase refers to ducks flying in formation, or in a shooting gallery at a fair. So, whether on the ground, in water or airborne, the reference is to organization.

USE & ABUSE:

This phrase has become a lodestone for loathing all things bull-related. As a lazy and overused metaphor for getting your shit together, it is harmless enough. And yet, few can shift the childish image of a plastic duck in a bathtub, and this has a curious ability to undermine the credibility of any boss who says it. Widely-derided, given its apparent innocence.

BULLSHIT-FREE VERSION:
Get organized.

> *"We need to sort everything out, right now."*

BULLSHIT RATING:

5.3: **END OF PLAY**

> *"I need that report without fail by the end of play."*

ORIGIN:

The end of play originally referred to the end of a sporting fixture — literally, the moment when play has finished. It has now morphed into a much vaguer term meaning the end of the working day, and that can be open to significant misinterpretation. The acronym EOP is now common in email conversations too.

USE & ABUSE:

This phrase is open to abuse by both the instructor and the receiver of the request. 'I'd like that by the end of play,' vs. 'I'll get that to you by the end of play.' Whoever says it, it is open to a very wide range of interpretation, ranging from 5.00pm for some to 11.59pm for others. Any boss using this phrase should be aware that they don't know when it will be done, and it could easily be tomorrow, not today.

BULLSHIT-FREE VERSION:
By 5 o'clock. *

> *"I would like that by 5 o'clock, please. Can you do it by then?"*

BULLSHIT RATING:

*Specify a precise time.

5.4: **SQUARE THE CIRCLE**

> *"You need to square the circle on this, Mike."*

ORIGIN:

Squaring the circle was a conundrum set by ancient mathematicians obsessed with geometry. The challenge is to construct a square with the same area as a circle, using a finite number of steps, with a compass and a straight edge. It's impossible. Some smart arse somewhere then adopted the phrase as a synonym for coping with a problem, overcoming it, or carrying off a neat trick.

USE & ABUSE:

The geometric origin of the phrase makes perfect sense. It can't be done, but at least we understand the challenge. Morphing this into an exhortation for hard-pressed executives is a supreme example of total bullshit. Literally, I would like you to complete a task that we all know can't be done.

BULLSHIT-FREE VERSION:
Do your best with a difficult task.

> *"I understand we often appear to ask for the impossible, but give it your best shot."*

BULLSHIT RATING:

5.5: STICK TO YOUR SWIM LANES

"You all need to stick to your swim lanes on this project."

ORIGIN:
In swimming, sticking to your lane is mandatory so as not to impede other competitors. Those who veer off are disqualified. Taking this as a metaphor for business organization, a so-called swimlane diagram is a flowchart that shows who does what on a project, with every employee, work group or department clearly separated.

USE & ABUSE:
The notion that employees should have a crystal clear view of what they're doing and avoid wasteful duplication of work has admiral intentions, in many contexts. There can, however, be two nasty side effects: 1) By being so clearly delineated, many departments simply ignore each other, leading to silos and, ironically, *increased* ignorance; 2) On leadership teams, those sticking to their lanes fail to contribute anything other than their specific discipline, leading to a lack of coherence at the top of the company.

BULLSHIT-FREE VERSION:
Don't duplicate work.

"Let's be totally clear about what each of us is doing."

BULLSHIT RATING:

6.
TEAM HUDDLES

Team huddles usually start with good intentions – to keep communication flowing, to make sure everyone knows what they are doing, and to increase efficiency. Sometimes it's a modest gathering by a pod of desks, sometimes a global check-in on Zoom.

But they can also be a hotbed of twaddle and bull. It really depends on the team leader, and how much motivational hot air they are inclined to trot out. If you're unlucky, such meetings will be full of exhortations to drill down, hit the ground running and jump on a call, unless everything is being put on the backburner, of course.

6.1: **BACKBURNER**

"We're going to put that on the backburner for now, Colin."

ORIGIN:

Known since the '40s, this one comes from the world of cooking. There are four burners on a conventional stove, so to put a pot on the back burner* is to relegate it to a position of less importance so the chef can concentrate on more pressing matters. In modern parlance, that applies to whether a project has priority or not. This should not be confused with the afterburners used to increase thrust on jet engines.

USE & ABUSE:

It's a bit of a daft phrase, but fairly harmless once the origin is known, and it appears to be universally understood as meaning to put something on hold for the moment. So, in that respect it fulfils its communication purpose. Interestingly, though, you will rarely hear someone say that we must bring something onto the frontburner, which suggests that a lot of projects are probably still languishing at the back of the company's metaphorical cooker.

BULLSHIT-FREE VERSION:
Do it later.

"That's not a priority, so we'll focus on what is."

BULLSHIT RATING:

Backburner (one word) and back burner (two) appear to be interchangeable. By definition, you can also have a frontburner or front burner.

6.2: **DRILL DOWN**

> *"We need to drill down and learn more."*

ORIGIN:

The origin of this word pairing is no more complicated that it sounds. It comes from mining or oil extraction, and simply means that the further you drill down, the more you are likely to discover. In business, it is a request to move from broad summary information to specific detail.

USE & ABUSE:

There will be plenty of occasions when it is appropriate to ask for more detail. Indeed, many a boss has been hoodwinked by merely concentrating on the so-called big picture without really knowing what is going on in their business. In the wrong hands, the tone of this instruction can be overly macho, conjuring up visions of burly men with pneumatic drills ripping up concrete. At its worst, though, it is used as a noun: "Send me the results of the drill-down, Richard."

BULLSHIT-FREE VERSION:
Provide more detail.

> *"We need more detailed information before we can make a decision."*

BULLSHIT RATING:

6.3: HIT THE GROUND RUNNING

> "We need to hit the ground running on Project Pot Plant, team."

ORIGIN:
This is a fascinating one, and hotly disputed. Theories include troops being dropped into a combat zone from helicopters, stowaways jumping off freight trains just before they enter a station, and Pony Express riders avoiding delay when changing horses. The military version is usually seen as the most plausible and has been common since the '80s. One way or another, it aims to convey that we need to be ready immediately to do whatever it is we're doing, and be effective right from the start.

USE & ABUSE:
The intent of the phrase here seems pretty clear — be prepared to spring into action. The Marines are acknowledged masters of preparation followed by immeasurable periods of waiting, and they have a saying: "Get ready and wait." Abuse is another case of context and tone – if the team leader favours the military metaphor, then this one could get a bit annoying, but the harm level feels relatively low.

BULLSHIT-FREE VERSION:
Be prepared for action.

> "When we start, we'll do it at full speed." ✓

BULLSHIT RATING:

6.4: **JUMP ON A CALL**

> "Let's jump on a call next week."

ORIGIN:
When the author was researching this, he was delighted to find his own definition at the top of 763 million references on a popular search engine. It reads: 1) Join a conversation on the phone. 2) Strangely energetic phrase suggesting that stringent physical action is somehow involved in the simple business of having a chat; a close cousin of jumping on an email, which sounds positively inadvisable. Nobody seems to know where this daft phrase came from.

USE & ABUSE:
People really hate this one, but in truth it's pretty harmless. The jump element suggests some form of enthusiasm or energy for the conversation, which could be a positive thing. But, because jump is a physical verb, it has no relevance at all to a conversation. This is a close cousin to other phrases, such as jumping in the shower and hopping on a bus, none of which are physically advisable. Annoying, yes, but hardly as dangerous.

BULLSHIT-FREE VERSION:
Talk on the phone.

> "Let's have a phone conversation about that." ✔

BULLSHIT RATING:

6.5: **TOUCH BASE**

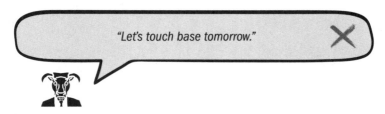

"Let's touch base tomorrow." ✕

ORIGIN:
In baseball, there are three bases and a home plate where the batsmen stand. Once the ball is struck, the running batsmen must touch the next base in order not to be declared out. American businesspeople then took it upon themselves to say that they must touch base – a euphemism for having a meeting or conversation at some point or renewing a contact.

USE & ABUSE:
One would have thought that everyone knows what this phrase is trying to convey, but interestingly there are over 500 million search requests for it online, so a lot of people clearly don't know. This is an example of one of those pat expressions that slips into office language, after which we find that some people don't even understand it. Bewildered colleagues then return to their desks wondering why their team leader was drivelling on about touching a bass guitar or something.

BULLSHIT-FREE VERSION:
Talk.

"Let's meet tomorrow." ✔

BULLSHIT RATING:

7.
HUMAN
RESOURCES

This is a rather odd word pairing. We are all human, but are we resources? Many would not wish to be regarded as such, and certainly not treated as a resource. In days gone by, this would have been called the personnel department. It then became HR, and in some companies is now called Talent Management.

No matter. This can be a very strange world, spanning the nasty divide between hiring and firing, between promotion and demotion, appraisals, staff disputes, and all points in between.

So whether you're leaning in to hot desking or facing an unprecedented war for talent, stand by for some constructive feedback.

7.1: **HOT DESKING**

"Gather round, guys. You'll all be hot desking from now on."

ORIGIN:

Somewhere back in the nineties, a trend arose in which workers were not given an allocated desk – they just sat wherever space was available. The term probably morphed from hot racking, which is a maritime expression referring to sailors with different shifts sharing the same bunk. Presumably from time to time the bunks did get hot, although a hot desk sounds somewhat uncomfortable.

USE & ABUSE:

The benefits of hot desking in an open plan office include enhanced teamwork, an increase in spontaneous conversations, and a generally busy atmosphere. There are however many disadvantages, including an inability for staff to have their own space, the constant need to carry personal effects everywhere and fiddle around with storage lockers, and days where you can't actually find anywhere to sit at all. More devious companies have even used the practice to save vast amounts of money on office space, deliberately not having enough desks for the number of employees – a gamble on staff morale if ever there was one.

BULLSHIT-FREE VERSION:

Sit where you can.

"You'll have to grab a desk wherever you can find one."

BULLSHIT RATING:

7.2: **LEAN IN**

> *"From now on, it's essential that we all lean in to change."*

ORIGIN:

This trite little instruction was coined by Sheryl Sandberg, Chief Operating Officer of Facebook, in the title of her 2013 book, *Lean In: Women, Work and the Will to Lead*, co-written with Neil Scovell. It means to grab opportunities without hesitation, and immediately became a rallying cry for empowerment in business.

USE & ABUSE:

Encouraging people to take opportunities that come their way is sound advice that dates back to Roman times — *carpe diem*, seize the day. Unfortunately, these days you're apparently supposed to 'lean in' to absolutely everything, and those who don't are accused of being uncooperative and resistant to change. It is also a linguistically odd instruction inasmuch as it would be irritating indeed if everybody were leaning into everything, including other people.

BULLSHIT-FREE VERSION:

Take opportunities.

> *"If you spot an opportunity, take it."* ✔

BULLSHIT RATING:

7.3: **SHIT SANDWICH**

"I went for my appraisal and they gave me a shit sandwich."

ORIGIN:

The technique behind this phrase was popularized by Ken Blanchard, author of The One Minute Manager series. The proposed method was to start the conversation with a compliment, then deliver the bad or unfavourable news, and then finish with another compliment. Word soon got around of this approach, not least because the book was a huge best seller.

USE & ABUSE:

A balanced appraisal can be a good thing, assuming it's true and fair. The shit sandwich is, however, deceitful, particularly if the appraiser has to make up the compliments purely to cushion the blow of some heavy criticism. The breathless advice proposing one-minute goals, one-minute 'praisings' and one-minute reprimands smacks of management on the fly, with only cursory attention paid to the appraisee. Nasty stuff.

BULLSHIT-FREE VERSION:
Candid feedback. *

"I am going to give you some honest comments about your work."

BULLSHIT RATING:

*Without the bullshit compliments.

7.4: **UNPRECEDENTED**

> *"Due to these unprecedented circumstances, we will be making redundancies."*

ORIGIN:

Unprecedented means without previous instance; never before known or experienced; unexampled or unparalleled. It was first recorded in 1615 and stems from precedent, as in precede, or 'to come before.' In straightforward language, this word literally means that the event or item has never been seen or experienced before.

USE & ABUSE:

This is a perfectly decent word that has suffered much abuse in recent times. Used in the correct context, it is fine. These are the very rare occasions where something really could not have been foreseen. In modern times, though, this is rarely true. Even the worldwide pandemic was predicted – in fact, it was even modelled to anticipate its likely effects. More and more people are claiming that things are unprecedented when they probably aren't to get themselves off the hook, so sadly the word has now become a euphemism for being caught on the hop, often having ignored warnings beforehand.

BULLSHIT-FREE VERSION:
Caught by surprise.

> *"We didn't see this coming."* ✔

BULLSHIT RATING:

7.5: **WAR FOR TALENT**

"We are determined to win the war for talent."

ORIGIN:

This ludicrous phrase was coined by Ed Michaels, Helen Handfield-Jones and Beth Axelrod as the title of their 2001 book, *The War For Talent*.[12] This was based on a McKinsey study that rather breathlessly likened the process of hiring decent staff to some kind of pitched battle in which desperate businesses were trying to kill each other over potential recruits.

USE & ABUSE:

Hiring high-quality employees is patently a good idea — if your company reputation is good and you have sufficient funds. But the idea that doing so is some kind of war is errant twaddle that takes the military metaphor another step toward utter bullshit. It conjures up visions of besuited Wall Street executives brandishing swords and shields, fighting running battles in the corridors of Manhattan.

BULLSHIT-FREE VERSION:

Process of hiring the best staff.

"Let's hire the best people we can find."

BULLSHIT RATING:

8.
APPRAISALS

Appraisals are a double-edged sword. Staff want them so they can at last get some proper comment on their work having been ignored all year. But sometimes, the conversations are exasperating.

Stand by to talk about whether you have enough of a can-do attitude, or the bandwidth to cope with your role.

It will be a 360° experience that examines your multitasking skills and examines whether you have the skills to square the circle.

8.1: **BANDWIDTH**

> *"Do you have the bandwidth for this?"*

ORIGIN:

Bandwidth is the maximum amount of data that can be transmitted over an internet connection or down a cable — literally, the width of the band through which the data or signal flows. In recent years it has become an analogy for the amount of brain capacity or time someone can spend on a task or project.

USE & ABUSE:

If used in connection with a cable or an internet connection, bandwidth is the correct term and makes perfect sense. When used in relation to brain capacity, it becomes much vaguer. The processing capacity of the conscious mind is 120 bits per second. To understand one person talking to us, we need 60 bits, so we can only cope with 2–3 things at once. So, a person could genuinely have insufficient bandwidth if bombarded with too much at once. That's attention capacity, but the word is also sometimes used to refer to intelligence, as in *"I don't think he has the bandwidth for this difficult task."*

BULLSHIT-FREE VERSION:

Time and resources.

> *"Do you have the capacity to pay proper attention to this?"*

BULLSHIT RATING:

8.2: **CAN-DO ATTITUDE**

"Well done, Laura. You have a really can-do attitude."

ORIGIN:

The can-do element refers to the notion that, when someone is asked if they can do something, they say they can do it. 'Can do' was popular in the Royal Navy in the First World War. The attitude part means disposition or feeling (someone's mental approach), but can also apply to a physical position, such as a stance or posture in ballet. The phrase has come to the fore in the last decade or so.

USE & ABUSE:

Everyone loves positivity, especially bosses, so in appraisals employees are often congratulated for having a can-do attitude. There are, however, two negative aspects of it. The first is that people with a relentless can-do attitude frequently take on far too much, never say no, and end up self-destructing under the workload. The second is that bosses just keep asking for more. As the old saying goes, as soon as you achieve the impossible for your boss, they simply add it to your regular list of duties. Individuals need to be realistic, make sure that they don't overpromise and underdeliver, and absolutely stop short of lying about whether they can get something done or not.

BULLSHIT-FREE VERSION:
Positive approach.

"Laura has a really positive and constructive attitude."

BULLSHIT RATING:

8.3: MULTITASKING

> *"Rob, you are brilliant at multitasking."*

ORIGIN:
The word multitasking first appeared in a 1965 IBM report describing the capabilities of its latest computer. In other words, it can perform multiple tasks. The notion was then applied to humans, with the suggestion that those who could do this were more talented and useful as employees than those who could not. By the 21st century, the world was awash with self-help books espousing the virtues of multitasking.

USE & ABUSE:
Being able to cope with a lot at once may be something of a virtue, but only up to a certain point. Those claiming to be good at multitasking wear it as a badge of honour, usually with a heavy dose of martyr syndrome, as in: "Aren't I brilliant? I'm so stacked with work." Sadly, studies now show that multitasking doesn't work because too many of the tasks are started but not finished. Even worse, those who claim to be best at multitasking turn out to be the worst. A better approach is rapid sequential tasking – start something, then don't start anything else until you have finished that one thing.

BULLSHIT-FREE VERSION:
Good at juggling many tasks.

> *"You are good at handling a lot at once."* ✔

BULLSHIT RATING:

8.4: **TAKE IT OFFLINE**

> *"Let's take this conversation offline."*

ORIGIN:

At first glance this would appear to make a distinction between a conversation that is online and one that is offline, but that's not where it came from. The line in question is the telephone line, and the idea that, cold war style, someone might be listening in to a conversation that should be private. So, the phrase actually means that there will be no further discussion on this topic now but that there will be later in a different context because the current one isn't suitable.

USE & ABUSE:

There will certainly be times when an issue is inappropriate for the context, which could be the theme of the meeting, or the combination of people present, so a deferment may be wise. Thoughtful bosses will do this to ensure that remarks are relevant to a meeting's topic, so that people aren't bored by irrelevant material, or to acknowledge sensitive subjects that should be handled privately. On the negative side, Machiavellian managers who don't want to be put on the spot will use it as a deflection technique to avoid an uncomfortable topic.

BULLSHIT-FREE VERSION:

Talk about it another time.

> *"I don't want to comment on that in front of other people, so let's have a separate conversation about it later."*

BULLSHIT RATING:

8.5: 360° APPRAISAL

> "We are taking a 360° approach to appraisals this year."

ORIGIN:

The idea of a 360° approach dates back as far as the 1950s when it was used at Esso, although there is no particular evidence that it was called 360° at that point. One version of it applies to views taken from every type of employee who interacts with the individual – subordinates and colleagues as well as the boss. It is called 360° because it looks at all points of the compass. Another version produces a circular map with a wheel of attributes, showing what the person is good and bad at.

USE & ABUSE:

In the old days, your boss told you whether you were any good or not, and that was that. The 360° approach was an admirable attempt to gain a fuller picture, although it remained a moot point as to whether the boss would truly take those other views into account. At their most flabby, 360° appraisals can be somewhat bland and vague. At their worst, promotion or a pay rise can be blocked by an anonymous contributor, leading to resentment all round.

BULLSHIT-FREE VERSION:
Balanced and wide-ranging assessment.

> "We'll collect a broad set of opinions and form a complete picture of your performance."

BULLSHIT RATING:

9.
TEAM
BONDING

Team bonding is a phrase in its own right, with the second word suggesting some sort of gluing together. Companies are awash with horror stories of 'offsite awaydays' in which gangs of executives in strange off-duty clothing are humiliated by a range of exercises such as falling backward into the arms of their colleagues or frantically building spaghetti towers.

Representatives of HR will doubtless be exhorting everyone to reach out to each other, walk the walk and sing from the same hymn sheet, whilst reassuring them that they have got their back.

9.1: GOT YOUR BACK

> *"Don't worry, guys, we've got your back."*

ORIGIN:
This phrase originates from the Second World War. As buildings were cleared by squads of soldiers, the first person in needed to have their back protected from enemy fire by their fellow troops. In peace time, this has come to mean to be willing and prepared to help someone when they need assistance, or back them up psychologically.

USE & ABUSE:
Supporting colleagues with physical work or backing up their position so that they are not subject to abuse is a fine thing. However, once again the military metaphor has run out of control here. This phrase invokes battleground imagery, with the implication that making a presentation or having difficulty with a colleague is somehow analogous to storming the barricades or fighting in the trenches. Breathless exaggeration, and unnecessarily over the top, but hardly damaging.

BULLSHIT-FREE VERSION:
You have our support.

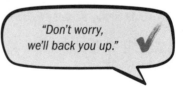

> *"Don't worry, we'll back you up."*

BULLSHIT RATING:

9.2: REACH OUT

"I think you should reach out to Jenny on this."

ORIGIN:

The first recorded version of this phrase is in a 1966 Four Tops song, *Reach Out (I'll be there)*. It then appeared in an ad campaign for the US phone company AT&T at the end of the sixties. The implication is that reaching out has an element of vulnerability and softness to it, in which the recipient of the contact can add an emotional, or even spiritual, component to proceedings.

USE & ABUSE:

In almost every context, this phrase just means to contact someone in some way. It has now become one of the most hated phrases in business — a truly horrible way of suggesting any form of interaction with a colleague or associate, offered in an 'arms around the world' sort of tone. For many, it conjures up visions of two fingers only just touching, as on the ceiling of the Sistine chapel, or a film villain about to drop off a cliff, despite vain attempts to hold them back. In conclusion, uttering these two words is only acceptable if sung by a member of the Four Tops.

BULLSHIT-FREE VERSION:
Talk to.

"Have a chat with Jenny about this."

BULLSHIT RATING:

9.3: SINGING FROM THE SAME HYMN SHEET

> *"We need to make sure we're all singing from the same hymn sheet here."*

ORIGIN:

A hymn sheet is a piece of paper with the words of a hymn on it, so the origin is religious. Variations include singing from the same hymn book, song sheet or sheet of music, and being on the same page. Should people not be, then the result will be a mess to listen to, and possibly impossible to understand. 'To operate according to the same plan or agreement, the same set of principles' – from British Industrial trade union parlance, possibly influenced by the Welsh choral tradition.

USE & ABUSE:

All saying the same thing has two rather different sides. 1) The message is clear, the team agrees with the management stance and message, and are happy to pass it on because they really believe it makes sense. 2) The message is vague or daft and no one likes it, so they slag it off, make up their own version or say nothing, leading to chaos and disruption. In an ideal world, people say the same thing in public as they do in the office, but it's pretty rare.

BULLSHIT-FREE VERSION:
Agree and portray a united front.

BULLSHIT RATING:

> *"We all need to agree and convey the same version to everyone else."*

9.4: **THERE'S NO I IN TEAM**

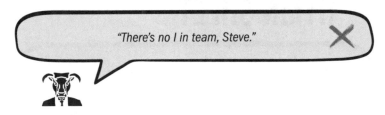

"There's no I in team, Steve."

ORIGIN:
The word team comes from Middle English and German and refers to a group of people pulling something along, such as a cart — something that one person alone could not do. The phrase is believed to have emerged in the sixties, in American sport, and is supposed to be a snappy mnemonic to remind those who like to fly solo that they shouldn't, and that they should work for the good of all rather than just themselves.

USE & ABUSE:
This is a much-derided phrase which most people dislike intensely as being trite and rather pathetic. Just because the letter I isn't in the word team is just fiddling around with letters. Critics point out that team does however include M and E, which spells me – the equivalent of I. All in all, it comes across as a rather trivial piece of semantic juggling with a few letters.

BULLSHIT-FREE VERSION:
Act for the collective good, not just yourself.

"Don't be selfish, Steve."

BULLSHIT RATING:

9.5: **WALK THE WALK**

> *"We can't just talk the talk, guys, we need to walk the walk."*

ORIGIN:

This means to do what you say you will. There are hundreds of variations, including practice what you preach, show me, don't tell me, and actions speak louder than words. It is frequently joined to talk the talk, the chatting bit that comes beforehand. Accurate origins are infuriatingly vague, with scores of references in American business from the '60s onward.

USE & ABUSE:

The underlying sentiment — that it is unacceptable merely to talk about something without actually converting the thought into action — is right and proper. Lack of action in this regard is hugely annoying. But then, so is the phrase, and most executives have rolled their eyes in a team meeting when the leader has intoned about talking the talk and walking the walk. It's essentially just a pat cliché.

BULLSHIT-FREE VERSION:

Enough talk, let's get on with it.

> *"We need to stop talking about it and get it done."*

BULLSHIT RATING:

10.
WATER
COOLER

A lot of shady conversations occur at the water cooler, itself a relatively modern import from the US. Before that, UK companies had a tap, a mouldy sink and a scale-encrusted kettle.

Grabbing some water or a coffee leads to all manner of side briefings, gossip and backstabbing – often called a water cooler conversation.

Stand by for a whole heap of moaning about the reorg, how everyone is working in silos, and someone's gut feel about the rumoured destaffing.

10.1: **BACKSTABBING**

> *"Mark has been backstabbing again – he's a total arsehole."*

ORIGIN:

This word is usually backstabbing as a noun (one word) and back-stabbing as an adjective (hyphenated). Although renditions vary, this one goes all the way back to Julius Caesar – in fact, to the invention of the knife.* It's impossible to pinpoint the date when the modern version of it emerged – to criticize someone behind their back whilst appearing to support them to their face.

USE & ABUSE:

It's very rare for someone to say in the first person that they are backstabbing, but almost everyone does it. The most extreme versions happen in short bursts of time: *"That was brilliant,"* said to the person in question. The moment they leave the room, the perpetrator turns to a colleague and says: *"That was shit."* More Machiavellian versions include appearing to support a boss and then actively briefing against them in order to get their job. It's a discussion point, but on balance frontstabbing is preferable – telling someone genuinely what you think to their face.

BULLSHIT-FREE VERSION:
Cowardly criticism when the person isn't there.

> *"I disagree with Mark, and I've told him so to his face."*

BULLSHIT RATING:

There is no evidence that he ever said "Et tu, Brute?" That was invented later for dramatic purposes.

10.2: **DESTAFFING**

"Due to poor sales, they say we will be destaffing."

ORIGIN:

This is no more complex than stealing the 'de' prefix and attaching it to the word 'staff.' One minute you have staff, the next the staff have been removed, or destaffed. Other awful examples include degrow, dejob, delayer and derisk.

USE & ABUSE:

There are no circumstances in which it is okay to use this word. Anyone who does is failing to acknowledge that they are talking about peoples' livelihoods. The first disgrace is to dehumanize the process of relieving someone of their employment by describing it as destaffing. The second is to insult the individuals in question by refusing to use plain language. Those using the word should be defenestrated.

BULLSHIT-FREE VERSION:
Making redundancies.

"People will be losing their jobs."

BULLSHIT RATING:

10.3: GUT FEEL

"My gut feel says we shouldn't be doing this."

ORIGIN:

The origins of this word pairing are pretty bizarre, when you think about it. It comes from the peculiar belief that emotions somehow emanate from the stomach* or gut area. Depending on the culture, this could also be the heart or the liver. These strange attributions of emotion to various parts of the body have been around since biblical times.

USE & ABUSE:

Use of this phrase is so ubiquitous that no one seems to notice how weird it is for people to be talking about their guts in business meetings. It's pretty revolting if you take it literally — I don't want to feel your guts, unless I am a doctor or an embalmer. In summary, a gut feel sounds both illegal and fatal. Consummate bullshit.

BULLSHIT-FREE VERSION:
Instinct.

"My instinct is that we shouldn't do this."

BULLSHIT RATING:

*Amazingly, some people believe they have butterflies in their stomach.

10.4: REORG

> *"Don't tell the troops, but we're looking at a reorg."*

ORIGIN:
Reorg is short for reorganization. The earliest recorded instances come from a 2006 book called *Managing Humans*, by software engineer Michael Lopp, and the fantastically titled "Purging Bloat to Fashion Sleek Software," a 2007 article in *The New York Times*.

USE & ABUSE:
A five-letter abbreviation may seem harmless enough, and perhaps it is. Yet, there is something hideously glib about it, particularly when uttered by supercilious management consultants or devious bosses. Whilst in theory a reorganization could be beneficial to all concerned, in practice they almost always lead to job losses and pain all round.

BULLSHIT-FREE VERSION:
Reorganization.

> *"We are changing the way the company is organized."*

BULLSHIT RATING:

10.5: SILOS

"We never speak to that department.
We're all working in silos."

ORIGIN:

The word silo comes from the Greek word *siros*, meaning corn pit.
The meaning moved across to military units, and then to systems and
departments that work in isolation. Synonyms include ghettos, buckets
and tribes. The rough idea is that businesses should strive hard to
prevent them happening, but they almost always do.

USE & ABUSE:

Conducting one's business affairs from inside a silage storage container
seems a pretty weird idea. This is actually a daft pseudo-agricultural term
to signal that everyone is doing their own thing and not talking to each
other — standard practice in most companies. It is even worse as a verb
or adjective, as in, "We don't want to silo the accounts department," or
"Production has really become siloed, don't you think, Jane?"

BULLSHIT-FREE VERSION:

**Departments that refuse
to interact.**

"We need to break
down departmental
barriers."

BULLSHIT RATING:

EXTERNAL
BULLSHIT

Next, looking outside companies, we work through the contexts in which they make their claims and interact with customers. Executives are under the spotlight in shareholder meetings, and when they make statements in annual reports and claims in advertising. Marketing and advertising meetings can be both internal and external – when brands interact with all the agencies and production companies that they hire to help them. Bullshit has also seeped horribly from the world of business into politics where those in a political fix use it to evade public scrutiny and wriggle out of tricky situations.

11.
SHAREHOLDER MEETINGS

Surely a contender for the biggest piece of fictional theatre outside the Hollywood film industry. Shareholders fill executives with dread because it is at these meetings that they are at their most vulnerable. Those who are members of the public cause havoc at the Annual General Meeting by decrying fat cat salaries and excessive boardroom largesse.

Meanwhile, venture capitalists just want their money back, fast, with a massive return on investment which they frequently don't get. So they use these meetings as a platform on which to humiliate the management and, on certain dramatic occasions, to stage a public coup and replace them with more compliant puppets.

11.1: **BAKED IN**

> *"Authenticity is thoroughly baked in to the brand's proposition."*

ORIGIN:

To bake is to cook by dry heat in an oven, and if something is baked in, then the ingredient is indeed inside the thing being baked – for example, a cake or pie. In recent times, baked-in as an adjective has been used to refer to something being built in, taken into account, or intrinsically included. It is invariably conceptual rather than physical.

USE & ABUSE:

This is a pretty poor phrase. The cooking analogy just about works to communicate that something should be an intrinsic part of the whole, but in the absence of any physical ingredients, use in a conceptual context almost always leads to lengthy pronouncements of utter bollocks. Nothing is actually baked in, and it's a moot point whether any shareholder would swallow this guff.

BULLSHIT-FREE VERSION:

A central ingredient.

> *"This is a crucial component in what we are doing."*

BULLSHIT RATING:

11.2: **GROUND-BREAKING**

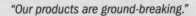

"Our products are ground-breaking."

ORIGIN:

A bit of an odd one, this, and it's been around since 1900. For a start, no one knows whether to write it as one word, two, or hyphenated. Whatever the form, the sense comes from the process of breaking ground at the beginning of any construction project, often accompanied by a short ceremony. Quite why or how this is a desirable quality in the generation of business ideas is a complete mystery. Literally, we would like some ideas that are similar to someone digging a spade into the ground.

USE & ABUSE:

This word is the subject of much confusion, especially in connection with its close cousin, breaking new ground. In architecture and engineering, the symbolism of physically starting a project can be very powerful and motivating. Unfortunately, the word ground-breaking has been hijacked as a lazy exhortation to do something new. So on closer inspection, we find that it doesn't really mean much at all other than new or different. Simply put, in what way should an intelligent idea bear any similarity to the first step in a building project?

BULLSHIT-FREE VERSION:
Inspired and genuinely original.

"We have some pioneering ideas."

BULLSHIT RATING:

11.3: **LEVEL PLAYING FIELD**

"We came a close second. It wasn't a level playing field."

ORIGIN:

This simply alludes to a sports field that gives one side an advantage if the pitch is on a slope and they are playing downhill. The first confirmed use of it was as recently in 1977, in a Pennsylvania newspaper, the *Tyrone Daily Herald*, by a lobbyist for the US Bankers Association. However, it probably dates back to a reference to being 'on the level' in George Burnham's *Memoirs of the United States Secret Service*, published in 1872.

USE & ABUSE:

Whilst the idea of things being fair is perfectly reasonable at face value, the phrase disguises two undesirable traits in business. The first is that most companies that fail to win a contract complain that it was not a level playing field — essentially a euphemism for losing. The second is that, with the same breath, businesses desire an 'unfair advantage.' Executives are schizophrenic on the issue of winning because they claim they crave a fair fight whilst also wanting to win at all costs, including a bit of cheating if necessary. This sporting analogy is of limited use.

BULLSHIT-FREE VERSION:
A completely fair contest.

"Let's win the business fairly, without resorting to underhand tactics."

BULLSHIT RATING:

11.4: **PARADIGM SHIFT**

"We are creating a paradigm shift in the market."

ORIGIN:

This rather scientific sounding phrase refers to a radical change in beliefs or theory. It was coined by US science philosopher TS Kuhn in his hugely influential 1962 work, *The Structure of Scientific Revolutions*. A paradigm is defined as a conceptual scheme. It provides scientists with their basic assumptions, concepts and methodology, giving their research its general direction and representing an exemplary model of good science in any particular discipline.

USE & ABUSE:

If a scientist or scientific community does indeed revolutionize or shift thinking in a certain field, then the phrase is appropriate. But this is almost never the case in business, so it is usually bullshit trying to glorify more modest achievements. More likely, it is precisely the same old shit we've always done, with no real change at all, or a minor difference pathetically trumpeted as a brave new dawn.

BULLSHIT-FREE VERSION:
A new way of doing things.

"We have a brand new perspective on the market."

BULLSHIT RATING:

11.5: **SKIN IN THE GAME**

> *"To be sufficiently committed to what we're doing, you need to have skin in the game."*

ORIGIN:

This curious phrase comes from the world of horse racing. Racehorse owners in the US were said to have skin in the game — with the skin in question belonging to the horses. As the owner, they had the most riding on the outcome of the race. The saying has also been attributed to the investor Warren Buffett, referring to investing in his own fund.

USE & ABUSE:

When the origin is explained, the phrase makes a certain amount of sense. But given that this author only discovered this when researching this book, it is probable that many don't really know what it means. It probably communicates the need for a vested interest, but without this knowledge it sounds more like the frankly mind-boggling principle that one might embark on a game that involves flaying oneself in some way, or perhaps gluing a part of your epidermis to another person.

BULLSHIT-FREE VERSION:

Have a vested interest.

> *"Make sure they have sufficient incentive to remain motivated."*

BULLSHIT RATING:

12.
ANNUAL
REPORTS

There is a stage management element to annual reports that allows the authors to choreograph what they want to say without interruption (unlike a shareholder meeting). You might think that the ability to prepare calmly and choose words carefully would lead to clearer communication.

But it doesn't necessarily happen. Bullshit creeps in everywhere, and it is perfectly possible to read a company's annual report and be none the wiser about the true state of its operations.

12.1: BIG PICTURE

> *"The role of the board is not to become bogged down in the minutiae. It is to see the big picture."*

ORIGIN:
There is no proven origin for this phrase, but a distinction is undoubtedly being made between something that is big and something that is small. The implication is that small is bad, which is a hell of an assumption. Probably invented by a bragging Texan.*

USE & ABUSE:
Merely considering the big picture whilst ignoring the detail could be disastrous, but then, so could the opposite. Micromanagement has left many a company or team failing to see what was coming over the horizon. The most insidious use of the phrase is when it is used personally, as in, "The problem with Martin is that he never sees the big picture."

BULLSHIT-FREE VERSION:
The complete view.

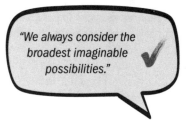

> *"We always consider the broadest imaginable possibilities."*

BULLSHIT RATING:

* *Old Joke. Texan: "Where I come from, I can drive all day and still be on my own land." Englishman: "Yeah, I had a car like that once."*

12.2: **BLUE SKY THINKING**

> *"Our technical specialists have embarked on a lot of blue sky thinking this year."*

ORIGIN:

This is roughly defined as brainstorming with no limits. The blue sky is a metaphor for being able to see a long way without obstruction, conveying the idea of unfettered thinking. But the original meaning of blue sky is much more specific, and quite different. In the early 20th century, blue sky was used to describe fraud. Unscrupulous financiers were described as inflating securities based on nothing more than 'blue sky and hot air.'

USE & ABUSE:

Blue sky thinking broadly communicates thinking without limits, and the notion that one idea leads to another has some merit. It is just about tenable that even the most ludicrous and impractical idea could trigger a better, more viable thought. On the negative side, many brainstorms are fruitless sessions full of pointless twaddle that will never see the light of day, and the suggestion that blue sky thinking is acceptable is a major culprit.

BULLSHIT-FREE VERSION:
Unfettered thinking.

> *"We have been thinking as broadly as possible, trying not to be constrained by current conventions."*

BULLSHIT RATING:

12.3: STATE OF THE ART

> "We have state of the art products."

ORIGIN:

The earliest use of the term state-of-the-art (hyphenated) dates back to 1910, from an engineering manual by Henry Harrison Suplee, a graduate of the University of Pennsylvania. It was rivetingly titled, *The Gas Turbine: progress in the design and construction of turbines operated by gases of combustion.* Ironically, the art in question is actually science. In short, the phrase refers to the stage that current expertize has reached, from technology to medicine, or any type of product or service.

USE & ABUSE:

To say that this is the current state of what we have seems perfectly reasonable. But the most common context these days is to use this term as an adjective, as in 'state-of-the-art products.' Suddenly, the suggestion is that these are the best ever, world beating, the latest in high-tech, etc. In other words, it's puffery to claim brilliance where there may be none.

BULLSHIT-FREE VERSION:
The best possible.

> "We have the best products that modern expertize allows."

BULLSHIT RATING:

12.4: **THOUGHT LEADERS**

> *"We are thought leaders in the industry."*

ORIGIN:

This term was coined by Joel Kurtzman, editor of *Strategy & Business* magazine, in 1994.[13] "A thought leader is recognized by peers, customers and industry experts as someone who deeply understands the business they are in, the needs of their customers and the broader marketplace in which they operate," he wrote. "They have distinctively original ideas, unique points of view and new insights."

USE & ABUSE:

Having an intelligent viewpoint is clearly a benefit, but there is a hidden bluff behind this concept. A market leader can demonstrate tangible success through having the biggest or most profitable sales. Those who cannot simply bang on about being so-called thought leaders. In other words, if we are not a leader, at least we can think and talk like one, even if it's not true. No one has ever shown the benefit of being a thought leader, probably because there isn't one. Absolute twaddle.

BULLSHIT-FREE VERSION:
Considered commentators.

> *"We have an interesting perspective on our industry."*

BULLSHIT RATING:

12.5: **TIPPING POINT**

> *"The market has reached a tipping point and we intend to take full advantage."*

ORIGIN:

This phrase started in physics, where it referred to adding a small amount of weight to a balanced object until it suddenly toppled or tipped. The sociologist Morton Grodzins then adopted it when he studied racially integrating American neighbourhoods in the 1960s. He discovered that most white families stayed as long as the comparative number of black families remained small. At a certain point, the remaining white families would move out *en masse* — something he described as white flight.

USE & ABUSE:

Using the phrase to denote the moment at which a phenomenon or craze 'tips' is reasonable enough, so long as it is applied in an appropriate context, but this is a widely abused term, found most frequently in the worlds of politics and public relations. On closer examination, it is usually a case of wishful thinking. In other words, we would like a tipping point in our favour, but no one really knows how to create one, so this is predominantly a retrospective term masquerading as a hope for the future.

BULLSHIT-FREE VERSION:
Moment when something really takes off.

> *"This phenomenon took off and we plan to capitalize on it."* ✔

BULLSHIT RATING:

13.
CORPORATE SOCIAL RESPONSIBILITY

Corporate Social Responsibility (CSR) is in itself a phrase that can cover a multitude of sins. The basic premise is good – hand over a proportion of your profits to good causes.

This is all well and good, but the even more noble approach for right-minded modern businesses is to build ethical practices into their business models so that charitable donation of time and money happens perpetually, rather than only if the company does well.

What companies claim in this area comes in many shapes and sizes, some of it with a healthy dose of bull. Stand by for brand ambassadors reminding you that we are all in this together and giving something back for maximum stakeholder engagement.

13.1: ALL IN THIS TOGETHER

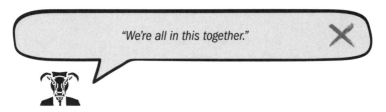

"We're all in this together."

ORIGIN:

This phrase is pretty much impossible to pin down. It is more of a sentiment rather than a specific, pat phrase. It variously turns up in songs, musicals and films, and as a unifying rallying call in political speeches as far back as Abraham Lincoln.

USE & ABUSE:

The thought that as a human race, a country or a unified group we are "all in this together" is broadly positive and motivating. Sadly, on closer examination, it patently isn't true. The world in total, and every society one looks at, is categorically not in this together. The gap between the rich and poor, whether by social strata or between countries, is disgracefully large. So there is a deep cynicism behind the phrase, especially when used by international brands patronizing their audiences and pretending that they care whilst doing bugger all to help people in tangible ways.

BULLSHIT-FREE VERSION:

Doing our bit.

"We are doing our best to help those less fortunate than us."

BULLSHIT RATING:

13.2: BRAND AMBASSADOR

> *"Our brand ambassador is a living, breathing personal manifestation of the brand."*

ORIGIN:

Originally, an ambassador was an accredited diplomat sent by a state to be its permanent representative in another country. Stick the word brand on the front and it morphs into a person, often a celebrity, who is paid to promote or endorse a company's brands, products or services.

USE & ABUSE:

Handled well, a sensitive and appropriately chosen brand ambassador can be a huge benefit to a brand, and a genuine force for good in the world. This assumes a responsible individual, a right-minded brand and suitable initiatives that are truly beneficial to people. That's nirvana, but boy, is this a fraught area. Major stumbling blocks include huge brands hurling vast amounts of cash at already-rich celebrities, cynical attempts to manipulate customers through disguised messages, and the high likelihood that the person in question will be caught *in flagrante delicto* with a hooker, face down in a drug den, or turn out to be a wife beater.

BULLSHIT-FREE VERSION:

Brand spokesperson.

> *"Our brand spokesperson represents what we're all about."*

BULLSHIT RATING:

13.3: GIVE SOMETHING BACK

> *"We feel it is essential to give something back."*

ORIGIN:

The original meaning of this phrase is to hand something back to someone after you have borrowed it. They give it to you, then you give it back. Simple enough so far, one might think, and that's how it was for hundreds of years. Then, suddenly, in a more touchy-feely world, it has come to mean to contribute to society in a constructive way rather than just exploiting every opportunity for monetary gain.

USE & ABUSE:

These three words look innocent enough and the broad sentiment is laudable, but there is something sinister lurking underneath. If you declare that you need to give something back, then it follows that you took it in the first place, so this is close to being an admission of guilt. There's more. True philanthropy can and should be conducted anonymously. The moment you crow about it, the more it looks as though this is a publicity stunt to boost your reputation. To be treated with extreme caution.

BULLSHIT-FREE VERSION:

We try to make a proper social contribution.

> *"We contribute appropriately to society because it's the right thing to do."*

BULLSHIT RATING:

13.4: STAKEHOLDER ENGAGEMENT

> *"We intend to ensure full stakeholder engagement."*

ORIGIN:
The word stakeholder was first used in 1708 to mean the holder of a wager or stake. A stake could refer to a wooden spike driven into the ground, or, more generally, 'that which is placed at hazard.' It then appeared in modern times in 1963, in an internal memorandum at the Stanford Research Institute. Engagement refers to having the undivided attention of whoever has stakes in the company or project.

USE & ABUSE:
If someone does indeed have a stake in the company, they are truly a stakeholder. But the phrase has been bastardized into meaning any Tom, Dick or Harry who wants to have a say in something, or a company that wants to engage with them. It is particularly abhorrent when manacled to another word, as in stakeholder interests, values, issues, and so on — all loose euphemisms for gaining the support of anyone with influence, and not pissing them off.

BULLSHIT-FREE VERSION:
Attention and involvement of influential parties.

> *"We want agreement with and approval from those who can influence our fortunes."*

BULLSHIT RATING:

13.5: **TRANSPARENCY**

> *"Here at Sunshine Desserts, we show complete transparency in all our dealings."* ✕

ORIGIN:

If something is transparent, you can see through it, so there's nothing hidden from view – literally, the light shines through it. Transparency has come to mean the condition of being transparent, as in openness. After hundreds of corporate scandals in which crucial facts and illicit activities hidden from the outside world were then exposed, the business community has become obsessed with the notion of transparency.

USE & ABUSE:

If you are doing the right thing, then being transparent presents no difficulty. And if that's true, then you don't need to point out that you are being transparent. Mention of transparency, therefore, almost always raises suspicion. The more you talk about it, the more people suspect a cover up. As such, the modern obsession with 'being transparent' is fraught and is often claimed without having any intention of shedding light on what the company gets up to at all. Shady dealings behind the scenes are often protected by a smokescreen such as a so-called CSR charter with no meat and no action.

BULLSHIT-FREE VERSION:
Openness.

BULLSHIT RATING:

> *"We are open to scrutiny and have nothing to hide."* ✓

14.
MARKETING

Desperate marketing has become a hallmark of modern life, with people being bombarded with thousands of messages every day. Generic products, generic marketing claims, and generic advertising creates a mush of general static that many pay little attention to.

Some of the language that goes on in marketing meetings hits the peak of bullshit heights, with talk of being top of mind, using all touchpoints and causing disruption. All of this spills out from the marketing department into meetings with the agencies they employ and the suppliers they work with.

Most important of all is to make sure that your campaign has real teeth.

14.1: **DISRUPTION**

> *"We need disruption to gain the attention of consumers."*

ORIGIN:

The root of this word is *disruptio*, a 15th century Latin medical term originally meaning laceration of tissue which then took on more general use as anything that was rent asunder, split apart, or shattered into pieces. In its modern form, it is less physical and more closely aligned with interruption, either to the status quo of an industry or regime, or an individual's time and attention.

USE & ABUSE:

Disruption could possibly be a good thing if a state of affairs has become too comfortable and is flawed. If so, breaking it up may be a positive move. But in a marketing context disruption has become a somewhat fatuous term for interrupting someone with a selling message – good for the advertiser but probably annoying for the recipient. Even worse is its bastard cousin abruption – abruptly interrupting someone. Whilst it makes breathless marketing folk believe that they are gaining someone's undivided attention, it is more likely that they are just pissing them off, which is why over 50% of people now block advertising online.

BULLSHIT-FREE VERSION:
Gain attention.

> *"We need to attract interest in an unorthodox way."*

BULLSHIT RATING:

14.2: BANG FOR YOUR BUCK

> *"This strategy will achieve more bang for your buck."*

ORIGIN:

This is a fun idiom from the USA. Bang is slang for excitement and the buck part is slang for an American dollar, so the phrase means to get full value for money for one's investment or effort. US Secretary of Defence Charles Erwin Wilson used it in 1954 to describe the proposed New Look policy of relying on nuclear weapons rather than a large regular army to keep the Soviet Union in check.

USE & ABUSE:

The basic principle of achieving good value for one's effort or investment makes good sense. The phrase itself, however, has some problematic areas. The bang element is somewhat dubious, possibly having sexual overtones and even hinting at a transaction between a man and a prostitute. The exact wording of the phrase shifts continuously, with versions including bang (singular) and bangs (plural), and bang for our/ your/the buck, as well as bucks gathering an S. The grandaddy of them all is *"More bangs for our bucks."*

BULLSHIT-FREE VERSION:

Decent return for investment or effort.

> *"This will provide excellent value for money."* ✔

BULLSHIT RATING:

14.3: **REAL TEETH**

> *"This campaign needs to have real teeth."*

ORIGIN:

The origins of this phrase are very hard to track down but we can nevertheless analyse it. Teeth are incisors and molars used for biting, chewing and eating. If a law has genuine power to compel obedience or punish offenders, it is said to have teeth – a metaphor for bite and authority. Real suggests not false but is really tautology – the unnecessary repetition of what is effectively the same idea – along the lines of effective effectiveness.

USE & ABUSE:

In a legal context, this phrase might just be acceptable, without the real part, to explain that a law has genuine power. But in a marketing context it is consummate nonsense. It is a close cousin of all the cutting based language such as cut through, cutting edge and so on. The closest one can get to expressing the sentiment clearly is to suggest that a campaign must have excellent effectiveness. And, of course, the teeth in question are patently not real, so this expression is simply another from the lexicon of desperate marketing people.

BULLSHIT-FREE VERSION:
Extremely effective.

> *"This campaign needs to be really efficient and successful."*

BULLSHIT RATING:

14.4: TOP OF MIND

> "It's vital that we are top of mind for consumers."

ORIGIN:

This curious anatomical reference means that something is a main concern or priority for someone. In its hyphenated form it preoccupies most people in marketing who are keen to promote so-called top-of-mind awareness – the notion that customers are always aware of their brand. References are hard to source, but have certainly been present in marketing circles since the eighties.

USE & ABUSE:

It is fairly understandable that over the years the head has been viewed as a receptacle for information, and that an analogy has developed suggesting that if a thought is at the top then it must come first. However, this reference is a lot more confused than it first appears. Variations include foremost and front of mind, and even the hideous front-of-mindness, but in truth no one seems to be able to work out whether it is preferable to be at the top or the front. All we know is that no one wants to be at the back, the bottom or in the middle.

BULLSHIT-FREE VERSION:
Highly regarded.

> "We want our customers to be considering us regularly." ✓

BULLSHIT RATING:

14.5: **TOUCHPOINTS**

> *"We must be present in all consumer touchpoints."*

ORIGIN:
This term evolved during the first 20 years of this century, in the world of media planning and buying. A touchpoint is business jargon for any interaction that a person has with a brand — before, during or even after they are a customer. It could be any form of contact, from advertising to a website or email. These interactions may be favourable or poor, such as good or bad customer service.

USE & ABUSE:
There is no doubt that marketing has become much more complex in the last two decades, so it is understandable that a nomenclature built up to explain it all. It is not uncommon for the number of a brand's touchpoints to exceed 200, for example. On the abuse side, the phenomenon has spawned an entire industry of jargon and impenetrable diagrams, usually some kind of wheel that looks like a terminally damaged spider's web. On balance, more baffling than genuinely harmful.

BULLSHIT-FREE VERSION:
Ways we interact with customers.

> *"We need a detailed understanding of all the ways we interact with customers, past, present and future."*

BULLSHIT RATING:

15.
ADVERTISING

As the need for sales becomes more imperative, the language used in briefings with advertising, public relations and so-called 'activation' agencies becomes more phrenetic and baffling.

Suddenly, everyone wants to win hearts and minds, cut through the clutter and ensure non-stop engagement with prospects and customers.

15.1: CUT THROUGH THE CLUTTER

> *"It's essential we cut through the clutter here, guys."*

ORIGIN:

Clutter comes from Middle English, with various forerunner versions such as clotter, cluster and clatter. It roughly means to gather in heaps, or crowd together, usually in a disorderly fashion. In advertising circles, 'the clutter' has become a euphemism for so many advertising messages that consumers don't see your ad or take any notice of it.

USE & ABUSE:

There is a deep irony in an industry generating so much material that it then has to cut through its own crap to be effective. Cut through comes in the form of a verb, but also the odious cut-through, a mutated verb-cum-noun. Overall, the whole thing involves a strange allusion to media messages somehow being physically tangible, so that you can cut them, as in, "We need to generate cut-through."

BULLSHIT-FREE VERSION:

Distinctive enough to be noticed.

> *"We need to do something noticeable and memorable."* ✔

BULLSHIT RATING:

15.2: ENGAGEMENT

"This is all about consumer engagement."

ORIGIN:
This word can mean so many things, from an appointment to preparing to get married to holding someone's attention. In an advertising context, the latter is the one they're going on about. The word comes from the French verb *engager* (to enlist in the army), but was then used more broadly as to encourage, sign up, hire, pledge or commit. This alternative use was first recorded in 1615.

USE & ABUSE:
Wanting to engage someone in a conversation is straightforward enough. It is the frenzied tone of advertising folk that drives this simple word to bullshit heights. They are obsessed with 'engaging the consumer' and 'driving customer engagement,' regardless of whether that is indeed what the audience wants. This type of engagement has nothing to do with an impending marriage, but simply refers to their paying sufficient attention to take action and buy something.

BULLSHIT-FREE VERSION:
Interaction.

"Let's make sure people pay attention to our message."

BULLSHIT RATING:

15.3: GAMIFICATION

"We'll use gamification to hook the customer in."

ORIGIN:
This term is said to have been coined in 2003 by Nick Pelling, a British computer programmer and inventor. The original purpose of it was to combine work with fun, based on the idea that work tasks can be made more appealing by turning them into a game. Since then, it has been adopted by numerous brands to make interacting with them more fun.

USE & ABUSE:
This is a tough one. Making something more interesting by turning it into a game seems innocent enough, depending on the context and the subject. However, gaming has a long history of addiction, and in many cases is tantamount to gambling. Silicon Valley even has a disgraceful term for technology so addictive that you can't even be bothered to go to the toilet: it's called a diaper product. Hooking your users in so comprehensively that they forget to relieve themselves, except while sitting right where they are, is cynical moneymaking twaddle.

BULLSHIT-FREE VERSION:
Presenting our product in a game.

"We have turned this into a game so that you get involved."

BULLSHIT RATING:

15.4: **HEARTS AND MINDS**

> *"We need to win hearts and minds."*

ORIGIN:

This phrase was first used by Louis Hubert Gonzalve Lyautey, a French general and colonial administrator, to refer to a method of bringing a subjugated population around to your way of thinking. It was part of his strategy to counter the Black Flags rebellion along the Indochina-Chinese border in 1895. It was then used by the US in the Vietnam War as part of their *Handbook For Military Support of Pacification*, and co-opted by the advertising industry to mean appealing both to feelings and logic. The heart represents emotion and the mind represents analysis of facts. The idea is that you need to win over both to secure a purchase.

USE & ABUSE:

This a horribly overused phrase to describe anyone paying any attention at all. The suggestion of linkage between brain and coronary apparatus has various flaws. There is no specific evidence that both emotion and logic are required in order for someone to buy something — many buy just on emotion, or just on logic. Aspiring to win over someone on both may therefore be completely unnecessary, or just plain unrealistic.

BULLSHIT-FREE VERSION:
Logic and emotion combined.

> *"Let's give our brand both rational and emotional appeal."*

BULLSHIT RATING:

15.5: NO SUCH THING AS A BAD IDEA

"There's no such thing as a bad idea, guys!"

ORIGIN:

This optimistic statement is much loved by those running brainstorm sessions, particularly in advertising and public relations. The brainstorm technique was invented by Alex Osborn (he was the 'O' in the famous advertising network BBDO) in 1953. It was designed to impress prospective clients by showing how creative they were in meetings. His philosophy was that freewheeling is welcome, and the wilder the idea the better, although there is no direct evidence that he ever said the phrase.

USE & ABUSE:

At face value, this phrase is complete rubbish; there undoubtedly is such a thing as a bad idea. That said, the sentiment that you can say what you like at least provides optimism, however unfounded, and the psychological safety to express one's views without fear of reproach. But the idea that all thoughts are welcome, no matter how poor, is pretty flawed, and essentially signals that we are incapable of distinguishing between a good idea and a bad one. In short, we don't care how much crap we generate, so long as it looks as though we're working, when in fact we are just eating biscuits.

BULLSHIT-FREE VERSION:
Be as imaginative as you can.

"We want intelligent, original thinking."

BULLSHIT RATING:

16.
SALES
PRESENTATIONS

Sales presentations can get very messy indeed, with wild claims and exaggeration just the starting point as different parties try to secure a deal. In a frantic push to a conclusion, you'll find the protagonists doubling down on their commitments, emphasising how much leverage they have, pushing the envelope and devising scores of ways to smash the competition.

16.1: **DOUBLE DOWN**

"We need to double down on this contract."

ORIGIN:

This phrase is found in a book on card playing by noted magician John Scarne.[14] In its original context of the card game blackjack, it describes a strategy whereby a player who is confident in their hand chooses to double their wager. In recent times, it has come to represent a redoubling of effort or commitment to get a deal done.

USE & ABUSE:

A quick search online shows that millions of people have no idea what this phrase means or where it comes from. Yet, these two simple words do roughly communicate a stepping up of effort, or a renewed burst of energy or commitment. On the abuse side, it is more vaguely used to mean going into something full throttle, chucking in the kitchen sink, or even overcompensating or overdoing it. In extreme cases, the salesperson in question flagrantly gambles with all their available resources, regardless of the consequences.

BULLSHIT-FREE VERSION:

Renewed and increased commitment.

"We need to dedicate more effort to this deal." ✔

BULLSHIT RATING:

16.2: ENTREPRENEURIAL

> *"We need to approach this deal in an entrepreneurial way."*

ORIGIN:
This word derives from the 19th century French verb *entreprendre* (to carry between), and took on a broader meaning of 'to undertake.' As a noun, it was used to refer to a middleman or intermediary. In modern times, it broadly means someone who is prepared to take risks in business or start one from scratch. It also implies a freethinking individual who isn't too interested in corporate rules or bureaucracy.

USE & ABUSE:
At face value, a salesperson who is prepared to take risks and be a self-starter should be applauded. But this is a tremendously overused term to describe anyone who runs their own business, or who has made a staggering number of cockups before getting it right, if at all. It is fairly harmless as a descriptor for any perfectly ordinary person running a business from home, but is at its worst as a smug and self-deluding personal introduction at networking meetings, as in "Pleased to meet you, I'm an entrepreneur!" Any salesperson behaving in an 'entrepreneurial' way may well be going against company policy and heading for the sack.

BULLSHIT-FREE VERSION:
Independent and imaginative.

BULLSHIT RATING:

> *"We need to take the initiative and be less corporate."*

16.3: LEVERAGE

> *"We can help you leverage your assets on this one, Steve."* ✕

ORIGIN:

The word leverage dates back to 1724, and was originally used to describe the action of a lever. By 1824, the Industrial Revolution was fully underway and the scope of the word had expanded to include the obtaining of mechanical advantage. Fast forward to the 21st century and it is used as both a noun and a verb to denote exploiting a situation to your advantage.

USE & ABUSE:

The engineering context of this word is absolutely fine and must always be a noun. Gaining leverage or, worse, leveraging something sounds horrible in the world of business. It is near-omnipresent in sales now, with people leveraging assets, situations, goodwill, competitive advantage — pretty much anything to win. The whole thing is built on the false notion that business is anything whatsoever to do with physics. It carries with it a suggestion of power and influence, but in truth is the last bastion of a cliché-ridden salesperson in full bullshit mode.

BULLSHIT-FREE VERSION:
Take advantage of.

> *"We can help you make the best of your strengths."* ✓

BULLSHIT RATING:

16.4: PUSH THE ENVELOPE

"With our product, we can really push the envelope."

ORIGIN:

This is from the world of aviation in the 1940s, meaning to push an aircraft to the limits of its performance capability in order to establish its tolerance levels. There is some suggestion that the original envelope in question was the structure containing the gas in an airship, but it could equally be that the expression comes originally from mathematics and engineering, where an envelope is a boundary. It was originally popularized by test pilots (especially those depicted in Tom Wolfe's book *The Right Stuff*) and it suddenly became popular again in the 1990s to mean testing limits and trying out new, often radical ideas.

USE & ABUSE:

The big problem with this phrase is that people use it without knowing what on earth it means. At face value, these words mean to move a piece of stationery across the table. So, really, it is another cracker from the kit box of sales executives who wished they had become a Top Gun pilot but never had the skill.

BULLSHIT-FREE VERSION:
Stretch boundaries.

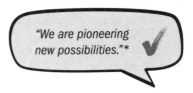

"We are pioneering new possibilities."*

BULLSHIT RATING:

*If it's true.

16.5: **UNFAIR ADVANTAGE**

> *"Our product will give you an unfair advantage in the marketplace."*

ORIGIN:

A quick search on the web for this term generates over 43 million references, but nothing on when or where the term was first used. It tends to mean something that a company owns or does that cannot be replicated by any other, giving them a near monopoly, and therefore significant advantage over rivals.

USE & ABUSE:

The huge flaw with this word pairing is that the word unfair is either redundant or plain illegal. An advantage is an advantage – plain and simple. If this has been achieved through nefarious means, then it is illegal. So, frankly, this is a bizarre phrase suggesting that winning can or should be achieved by cheating or somehow bending the rules, as though that were acceptable in business – a notion that raises the question as to why a fair advantage would not be equally acceptable. This is a pretty disgraceful phrase that sits alongside its deceitful cousins *Failure is not an option* and *Level playing field*.

BULLSHIT-FREE VERSION:
Advantage.

> *"Our product has a specific advantage over the others."*

BULLSHIT RATING:

17.
PRODUCT
CLAIMS

Pretty much every product manager or salesperson reckons that their product is brilliant, but this may or may not be true. Given that so many products are practically the same, many have little to shout about that is different or distinctive.

So, they make up whatever they can to snare a sale, whether that's droning on about bespoke solutions, key benefits and being with you every step of the way, or claiming to be game-changing, cutting-edge and more.

17.1: BESPOKE SOLUTIONS

"Here at Acme Plumbing we offer bespoke solutions."

ORIGIN:

Bespoke comes from early Middle English (before 900) and is the past tense of bespeak — to reserve beforehand or ask for in advance. It means specifically tailored for one customer. A solution is the state of something being solved, so at face value this phrase means something, or several things, solved specifically for one customer only.

USE & ABUSE:

This is one of the most hackneyed and lazy product claims ever invented. Solutions is a totally pointless modifier to almost any word, as in painting solutions (painters), marketing solutions (marketing), and even culinary solutions (food). These so-called solutions are in fact rarely bespoke at all, instead being a hotchpotch of already available elements hastily cobbled together, despite claims that they are tailored specifically to someone's needs.

BULLSHIT-FREE VERSION:

The product you need specifically designed for you.

"We will design and provide a product specifically adapted to your needs."*

BULLSHIT RATING:

*If it's true.

17.2: CUTTING-EDGE

> *"We have a range of cutting-edge technology products."*

ORIGIN:

As a noun, this is the sharp edge of something like a knife or similar tool. As a hyphenated adjective, it has come to mean the latest or most advanced stage in the development of something. Used since the 1700s, first versions may have applied to the plough rather than a knife.

USE & ABUSE:

This phrase may realistically be applicable to certain highbrow intellectual fields, such as those in science and engineering. For pretty much every other category, the claim comes across as a semi-industrial descriptor desperately trying to suggest that something is particularly advanced or ingenious, when it probably isn't. It's fine in highly sophisticated contexts, but not when referring to something perfectly straightforward, such as a bicycle or paper clip.

BULLSHIT-FREE VERSION:

The best that modern understanding allows.

> *"Our products are the most advanced available."*

BULLSHIT RATING:

17.3: **EVERY STEP OF THE WAY**

> *"We're with you every step of the way."* ✕

ORIGIN:
The origin of this precise phrase is fiendishly difficult to track down. The words are simple enough: someone is on some kind of journey, the steps get them from A to B in stages, and someone else helps them. It is now ubiquitously used by corporations that wish to retain a customer for life, to suggest that they have a product or service for every stage anyone might go through.

USE & ABUSE:
The sentiment behind this phrase is thoughtful and accommodating, if it's true. It is much favoured by banks but also purveyors of products for more fleeting moments such as baby products. However, abuse takes two forms. 1) It has been used so many times by so many companies that it has effectively lost its meaning, being so bland and generic. 2) There are thousands of examples where a company has made the claim and then let a customer down at one stage or another, thus undermining the entire basis of it.

BULLSHIT-FREE VERSION:
A product or service for every situation you might encounter.

> *"Whatever happens, we have a product or service to help."* ✓

BULLSHIT RATING:

17.4: **GAME-CHANGING**

"We have a game-changing approach to the market."

ORIGIN:

'Game changer' first appeared in the US sports pages in 1982. It refers to decisive plays in particular games that significantly changed their outcome, not to changes in rules or methods of play. The term then seeped into business jargon in the nineties and arrived in politics by the turn of the 21st century. It is now a catch-all phrase meaning anything brand new or revolutionary.

USE & ABUSE:

An inspired piece of play in a game can indeed change its outcome, so the term has a fair basis on which to convey something brilliant and unexpected. Viewed another way, this is an extraordinarily perverse piece of logic that suggests that if you can't win the game you're playing, you should move on to another game entirely. Quite how this helps anyone in business is a total mystery.

BULLSHIT-FREE VERSION:
Original and inspired.

"We have a highly original take on the market."

BULLSHIT RATING:

17.5: KEY BENEFITS

> "Look at the key benefits of our product."

ORIGIN:
Bene is Latin for good, so a benefit bestows an advantage on the recipient. In a product context, the benefits will be what the customer gains from buying the product or service. Key is a modifier suggesting that these are the most important benefits, but with the implication that there are others.

USE & ABUSE:
There is nothing particularly wrong with a brand wanting to outline what the merits are of purchasing it – that's just straightforward marketing. But there are three major flaws with this phrase. The first is that it is much more powerful to state what the benefits are without calling them benefits. The second is that often the list of them is so long that they cease to be 'key', or indeed obvious benefits. And the third is that the word key is horribly overused. The addition of key adds no increase in meaning at all, and simply serves to suggest that these benefits are important, but there are plenty of others that aren't.

BULLSHIT-FREE VERSION:
The main points.

> "The advantages of this product are A, B and C."

BULLSHIT RATING:

18.
CUSTOMER
SERVICE

Customer service is awash with bullshit, with companies incessantly claiming that their customers are revered deities at whose altar they worship. Sometimes, companies are indeed excellent at it, but there are millions of examples of customers who have been badly treated, ignored, or even ripped off.

It's the overclaim combined with the under-delivery that proves to be the unpleasant black spot. For some reason, companies want to exceed your expectations, go the extra mile, and tell you that nothing is impossible, 24/7. But is it?

18.1: GO THE EXTRA MILE

"Here at Broadbeam & Bandicoot, we always go the extra mile."

ORIGIN:

Under ancient Roman Impressment Law, a Roman soldier passing by a Jew could order him to carry his pack for one mile. How's that for racism and subjugation? In the Bible (Matthew 5:41) Jesus advises: "If a man in authority makes you go one mile, go with him two." The phrase was also present in a song by Joyce Grenfell in 1957. It is a vernacular cousin of exceeding expectations.

USE & ABUSE:

If people knew the appalling origin of this phrase, they would probably never use it. There is nothing wrong with a company claiming that they put in extra effort to make customers happy, so long as it's true. But there are limits. Constantly doing or delivering more than necessary for every customer will simply lead to bankruptcy. The metaphor itself is fraught, in that if you really did travel one mile further than necessary to reach your destination, you would presumably overshoot it in the process. Anyone genuinely doing so will not have arrived at their intended destination, but in fact somewhere entirely different.

BULLSHIT-FREE VERSION:
Do something extra.

BULLSHIT RATING:

"We deliver more than you expect."

18.2: **HANDS-ON**

> "We take a hands-on approach to customer service."

ORIGIN:

Hands-on (hyphenated) originally came into use in the 1960s, when it referred to the use of computers in education. Students would literally be encouraged to have their hands on their computer keyboard, to engage with the technology in front of them. In business it has come to mean highly attentive.

USE & ABUSE:

Being hands-on is patently double edged. Fans would say that having such an approach is great, but detractors would point to micro-management, control freakery and meddling. Claiming to offer a hands-on approach could be good if it gives the customer excellent service — if it's what they want, and if it's true. But that is often not what they want. For example, you don't want a hands-on relationship with your electricity provider, constantly harassing you. In that context, a hands-off approach is preferable.

BULLSHIT-FREE VERSION:
Always attentive.

> "We are involved in every aspect of customer service."

BULLSHIT RATING:

18.3: NOTHING IS IMPOSSIBLE

> "Here at Saatchi & Saatchi our mantra is that nothing is impossible."

ORIGIN:

On one level, this is a religious reference, with the Bible claiming in Luke 1:37: "For with God nothing shall be impossible." The phrasing is not identical, but the sentiment is. The actress Audrey Hepburn is also reported to have said: "Nothing is impossible; the word itself says I'm possible." A rather twee wordplay, but presumably intended to be motivational. In the 1980s, the advertising agency Saatchi & Saatchi chose the phrase as its clarion call, rather arrogantly suggesting that it could achieve anything.

USE & ABUSE:

There is nothing specifically wrong with the optimistic thought that we genuinely believe we can do anything, but what this phrase is really trying to say is that we often achieve what others may think is not possible. On close examination the phrase is utter rubbish. Given that time travel, unaided flight, the firing of mind bullets, and a vast array of other dreams clearly remain out of the reach of humans, it is patently untrue. In a customer service context, it could even spell disaster, given that plenty of things are indeed impossible. This phrase is a flawed bedfellow of *Think the unthinkable*.

BULLSHIT-FREE VERSION:
Inventive ways to succeed where others don't.

> "We have a reputation for achieving things that others say can't be done."

BULLSHIT RATING:

18.4: **PROACTIVE**

> *"We pride ourselves on taking a proactive approach."*

ORIGIN:

This word was originally coined in a 1993 psychology paper by Paul Whiteley and Gerald Blankfort, where it was used in a technical sense. If you are proactive, you make things happen, instead of waiting for them to happen to you. Active means doing something. The prefix 'pro' means before. So, if you are proactive, you are ready before something happens, as opposed to being reactive, where you only take action as a result of some other event.

USE & ABUSE:

A tendency to initiate rather than react is doubtless a desirable quality, but this word has been subjected to sustained abuse in the last 20 years. It has been an omnipresent adjective in the promotional material for advertising and PR agencies – as though a passive or reactive approach would be more appealing to customers. Now everywhere in politics, this is a redundant word, and a close contender for worst bull of the lot, along with going forward.

BULLSHIT-FREE VERSION:
Thinking ahead.

> *"We anticipate your needs and take the initiative."*

BULLSHIT RATING:

18.5: 24/7

> *"We'll be all over your contract, 24/7."*

ORIGIN:

The Oxford English Dictionary defines the term as "twenty-four hours a day, seven days a week; constantly." Apparently the first reference to 24/7 was from the US magazine *Sports Illustrated*, in 1983.[15] It was said by basketball player Jerry Reynolds, talking about his jump shot (when a player releases the ball in mid-air). Reynolds said his was "good 24 hours a day, seven days a week, 365 days a year." In business, it refers to services that are permanently available, or teams that never stop working.

USE & ABUSE:

This is another example of context and potential overclaim. If it is true that a service is constantly available, then the claim is fine. Most likely this would be something automated such as online. If humans are involved, then clearly they need to sleep, so the only way something could be delivered in person 24/7 is through carefully planned rotating teams. Often though, this three-numbered throwaway customer service claim is actually overclaim, as in *"We are dedicated to you 24/7."* Then nobody picks up the phone.

BULLSHIT-FREE VERSION:
Constantly.

> *"Our service is always available."*

BULLSHIT RATING:

19.
SLOGANS

There have been millions of slogans over the years. In advertising they are often called endlines or straplines. Ever since people started producing stuff, they've been trying to sell it. Those linked specifically to brands speak for themselves, and some rightly become famous.

Others have a generic theme – a sort of cliché that comes around time and again, appearing in a slightly different form each time. These are invariably lazy and generic and add little value to a brand.

This of course means that writing bullshit-free versions is almost impossible – without the brand name, the slogan writer has nothing to go on.

Here are five examples.

19.1: DESIGNED WITH YOU IN MIND

"Our products are designed with you in mind." ✕

ORIGIN:

Tapping this phrase into a well-known search engine immediately generates 1,700,000,000 results. It is applied to every type of business imaginable – showers, website creation, event planning, personalized gifts, home decoration, retirement homes, software, you name it. There is even a legal case in the US that has ruled against it being a registerable line, describing it as a "common informational message that fails to function as a service mark." It intends to convey that the product in question will suit your needs perfectly.

USE & ABUSE:

This is one of the laziest claims in the world. Attracted by the gentle rhyme of 'designed' and 'mind,' the copywriter cannot resist the cliché. In one or two highly upmarket cases, such as home interiors, it is just possible that the claim is true – that the design in question is unique to you. As for all the rest, it's complete bollocks. As the legal case suggests, it is unprovable, and in almost every case, palpably untrue. It also begs the rhetorical question: *"Well, who else would you have in mind when you designed it? Someone else, perhaps, but not me?"*

BULLSHIT-FREE VERSION:
Genuinely made for you.*

BULLSHIT RATING:

"We really do consider our customers in every step of the design process." ✓

*If it's true.

19.2: FOR ALL OUR TOMORROWS

"Our services will be here for all our tomorrows."

ORIGIN:

"For your tomorrows, they gave their today." The poet John Maxwell Edmonds produced this epitaph in his 1919 poetry. "Tomorrow's Technology Today" was coined by writer Norman Bergrun in 1972. "Today's science is tomorrow's technology" is a quote by Edward Teller, the American-Hungarian theoretical physicist, in his book *The Legacy of Hiroshima* (1975).[16] Thousands of corporate claims have offered endless permutations of yesterday/today/tomorrow over the years.

USE & ABUSE:

Fiddling around with time is a favourite of large corporations. They variously want you to know that: 1) they have been around for ages; 2) are right on the money today; and 3) will be here for years to come. The first is simply a matter of fact which anyone can check, the second is hard to prove, and the third is unknown. As a result of this, any statements based on today/tomorrow are, at best, conjecture. Companies collapse all the time. Since 2000, 52% of companies in the Fortune 500 have either gone bankrupt, been acquired or ceased to exist. So this is just corporate puffery.

BULLSHIT-FREE VERSION:
Moving with the times.

"Our aim is to be here for the long term." ✔

BULLSHIT RATING:

19.3: LOOK WHAT'S IN STORE

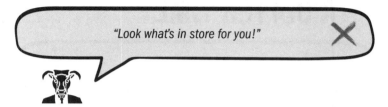

"Look what's in store for you!" ✕

ORIGIN:
In use in advertising since the 60s, but Edmund Spenser used this idiom in The Faerie Queene as far back as 1590: *"Then for her son . . . in her own hand the crown she kept in store."* Copywriters the world over have never been able to resist the word play between in store (a physical one where they sell stuff) and in store (something that will happen in the future).

USE & ABUSE:
Look what's in store for you! Geddit? It's in our store, and it's waiting for you some time in the future! Okay, we get the pun, now stop using it. As the high street declines, there are in fact fewer and fewer physical stores, so this line is becoming more and more redundant, as though it wasn't already. Weak and derivative.

BULLSHIT-FREE VERSION:
Look at our products.

"We have a lot of products you may be interested in." ✓

BULLSHIT RATING:

19.4: THERE'S NEVER BEEN A BETTER TIME

"There's never been a better time to buy."

ORIGIN:

This phrase has been in use for decades, with nearly 700 million different variations. There's never been a better time to... work in our industry, buy this product, take advantage of this offer, invest in these shares, and even, strangely, to die. The supposition behind the claim is that at no point in the past have conditions been so beneficial, so now is the moment to act.

USE & ABUSE:

Another in a long line of contradictory and patently unprovable claims. The first assumption is that there has never, ever, at any point in the past, been a more favourable moment in which to do this thing, whatever it is. That's a hell of a claim, and most likely untrue. The second is that there will never be a more advantageous time, at any point in the future, which is again something that we don't know. Even worse, the claim is frequently not backed up by any motivating reason to justify it. More vacuous tripe that simply doesn't stand up to scrutiny.

BULLSHIT-FREE VERSION:
A good moment.

"Now is a good time to buy, and here's why."

BULLSHIT RATING:

19.5: 9 OUT OF 10 PEOPLE AGREE

"9 out of 10 people agree that our product works best."*

ORIGIN:
Ever since the advent of commercial television in the 1950s, this type of pseudo-statistical claim has been rife. Medical endorsement was one of the first culprits, as in "Nine out of ten doctors agree." Scepticism began to increase with the publication of Darrell Huff's *How to Lie with Statistics* in 1954. Recommendations then bled into pretty much every advertising category, notoriously household washing products and cosmetics.

USE & ABUSE:
The biggest problem with any claim of this sort is the sample size. Extraordinarily, even TV ads in 2020 base claims on tiny sample sizes, typically of under 100, so the claims aren't even statistically valid. Nor is the nature of the respondents properly scrutinized, leading to the lingering suspicion that someone with a vested interest simply asked a few influenceable mates to say something nice for a few quid. And yet the claims keep coming. Surely it's time to retire this one on the grounds that no one believes it. Or do they?

BULLSHIT-FREE VERSION:
People really like this product.

"Our product is popular with a lot of people, and here is the evidence to prove it."

BULLSHIT RATING:

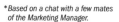
Based on a chat with a few mates of the Marketing Manager.

20.
POLITICS

And so we reach the widest public domain – politics. Politicians are now the undisputed champions of bullshit. It's partly down to their narcissistic tendencies, and partly down to context.

As Billy Connolly once accurately observed: "The desire to be a politician should bar you for life from ever becoming one." That's the glory seeking, power hungry part.

But it's often the context that gets them. They are in front of a microphone, they have twenty seconds, and they're trying to wriggle out of an unsatisfactory situation. And then they start talking...

There will doubtless be a proactive pursuit of key learnings going forward, leaving no stone unturned as they pass the buck.

20.1: **EXCEED EXPECTATIONS**

> *"Our policies are designed to exceed expectations."*

ORIGIN:
This phrase is broadly based on the notion that customers have some basic idea of what they can expect from a product or service, and that this can be exceeded by receiving something of additional benefit.

USE & ABUSE:
Expectations are by definition subjective – mine might be different from yours. Most customers quite rightly expect a product or service to do what it claims and deliver value for money based on the price paid. The higher the price, the higher expectations may be, but in truth these expectations are really just a diffuse set of things that consumers apparently 'expect' from a company. A true bonus on top of what you have paid for is a highly desirable thing, but often companies only aim to 'exceed' expectations when something has gone wrong. That's not exceeding expectations – it's desperately trying to put something right so that customer satisfaction is back where it should be.

BULLSHIT-FREE VERSION:
Something extra, without being asked.

> *"You'll be consistently dismayed by our failure to deliver what we have promised, let alone do more."*

BULLSHIT RATING:

20.2: GOING FORWARD

"We will learn from this going forward."

ORIGIN:

These two words are widely regarded as having come from Corporate America, and more specifically from the Securities and Exchange Commission, the US investment regulatory agency. Using words such as 'at some point in the future' or 'somewhere down the road' were regarded as too vague and lacking in authority, so 'going forward' became the default setting for anyone proclaiming on an uncertain topic. Literally, it means the opposite of backward.

USE & ABUSE:

Truly a king amongst kings – the undisputed champion of utter bullshit, with the possible exception of 'proactive'. This is an entirely pointless modifier somehow designed to suggest a forward-looking demeanour, when any fool knows that a backward one would be detrimental for everybody, except possibly historians who should indeed adopt a backward-looking approach.

BULLSHIT-FREE VERSION:*

*Deliberately left blank. These two words add no meaning at all.

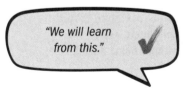

"We will learn from this."

BULLSHIT RATING:

20.3: **LEARNINGS**

"We will take the key learnings from this."

ORIGIN:

Learnings, with an 's,' has only appeared in the last 20 years. Prior to that, it was only singular. It has been around as a noun, referring to a thing learned, since the 14th century. The inference is that whereas people were originally happy to learn one thing, they now require several or many.

USE & ABUSE:

Learnings must be more than one piece of knowledge acquired. This is the grim plural of an active verb, suggesting intellectual progress on all fronts, where usually there is precious little, as in, "It's time we accumulated our learnings on Project Earwig, everybody." Even worse is 'key learnings.' There is no definition for this — learning is knowledge gained by study. There is no such thing as a key learning, nor several of them, unless it means learning how to use a key.

BULLSHIT-FREE VERSION:
Things we have learned.

"We have learned nothing and will doubtless cock it up again next time."

BULLSHIT RATING:

20.4: NO STONE UNTURNED

"Our investigation will leave no stone unturned."

ORIGIN:

This phrase, in its present form, originated in the mid-1500s. It is from an ancient Greek legend about a general who buried a treasure in his tent after being defeated in battle. Those searching for the treasure couldn't find it, and consulted the Oracle of Delphi, who advised them to look under every stone. Sound advice indeed, but debatable whether an oracle was needed to come up with the suggestion. It now means to look at everything that went on, usually as a post-mortem when something has gone wrong.

USE & ABUSE:

The idea of launching a thorough investigation into something when it has gone badly is admirable – once, and once only. The deep flaw in this phrase is that politicians do it again and again, learning bugger all in the process. Cock-up, repeat, cock-up, repeat. By now, we have every rock facing upward and nothing left that has not been investigated. Are we any the wiser? Apparently not. This phrase is much loved by politicians desperate to suggest that their efforts will be comprehensive, and to protect themselves from criticism from the opposition or the public. It is most commonly used when things have gone spectacularly wrong and someone has been rumbled.

BULLSHIT-FREE VERSION:
Everything thoroughly investigated.

"We will get someone who supports us to write a full report and then ignore the findings anyway."

BULLSHIT RATING:

20.5: PASS THE BUCK

> *"We will not pass the buck on this issue."*

ORIGIN:

Meaning to shift responsibility to someone else, this phrase derives from card games where a marker, or 'buck,' is put in front of the dealer to remind players who the dealer is. The original marker may have been a knife with a buckthorn handle or, in the Old West, a silver dollar. Hence, the modern use of the word buck for a dollar.

USE & ABUSE:

The idea that a person in a position of power will not shirk their responsibility by passing the blame onto someone else is a good thing. But, of course, that's not what usually happens. More likely, there will follow an outrageous abdication of responsibility, a total failure to live up to the job description, and an automatic raising of hands, as if to say: "Nothing to do with me!" The desirable alternative lies in its sister expression, 'The buck stops here,' popularized by US President Harry Truman, who kept a sign with that phrase on his desk in the Oval Office. In other words, 'I am fully responsible for everything, and am prepared to face the consequences.'

BULLSHIT-FREE VERSION:
Take full responsibility.

> *"We'll blame everyone but ourselves."*

BULLSHIT RATING:

"Truth is what my colleagues will let me get away with."
– Richard Rorty

PART THREE

WHAT TO DO ABOUT IT: A BULLSHIT NAVIGATION GUIDE

I. DEALING WITH BULLSHITTERS

TEN QUESTIONS TO ASK A BULLSHITTER

One of the best ways to deal with bullshitters is to question everything they say. Try some of these:

1. "Do you really believe that?"
   Leave a decent pause and see if they repeat it or change tack.

2. "Do you really mean that?"
   If they say yes, consider saying, "How extraordinary!" to make them look daft.

3. "What is the source of the information for that?"
   Put them on the spot to see if they have any evidence.

4. "Do you think that's a fair comparison?"
   To be used when they are conflating two very different things.

5. "This seems too good (or bad) to be true. Are you sure?"
   Highlight the unlikely nature of the extreme position they are taking.

6. "That figure seems inordinately high. Are you sure you have it right?"
   Put doubt in their mind. Perhaps they have slipped a decimal point?

7. "Have you considered more than one view about this?"
   Suggest a more open-minded approach to the subject.

8. "So what you are saying is 'X.' Is that right?"
Repeat back their bullshit with some plainer language.
See if they still agree.

9. "Can I just check that I heard those numbers correctly?"
Repeat them back, emphasizing the big ones incredulously.

10. "Have you always believed this or is this a newly held opinion?"
This flushes out those who repeat the last thing they heard on a subject.

TEN QUESTIONS TO ASK YOURSELF
This is how to question someone's stated authority by analyzing what
they are saying in your own head. Ask yourself:

1. Did they cite the authority correctly?
Check the source for accuracy.

2. Can that authority be trusted to tell the truth?
Check the source for validity.

3. Is the cited authority in fact an authority in the appropriate area?
Sometimes unqualified people comment on topics they
don't understand.

4. Is there agreement among appropriate experts on this issue?
Consensus is helpful. Disagreement suggests the view on this issue
is uncertain.

5. Why is an appeal to authority being made at all?
People often protest too much or cite bogus data.

6. Who is telling me this?
Do I trust the person saying this? What do they stand to gain?

7. Are they making unfair comparisons?
   They may be pulling random facts from different places to sound good or confuse an issue.

8. Is their claim too good or too bad to be true?
   Either extreme may reveal that the claim is false.

9. Is the order of magnitude of what they are saying likely to be true?
   Figures that seem ludicrously extreme are often just wrong.

10. Could there be multiple explanations here?
    Most things can be explained in different ways.

QUESTION THE NUMBERS

When bombarded by numbers that you suspect to be bogus, try asking: 'What do you mean: all, some, many or most?' This will flush out likely levels of exaggeration.

EXPLAIN YOUR FEELINGS

This is a formula from Thomas Erikson's book, *Surrounded By Psychopaths*, for dealing with a manipulative bullshitter. If they are trying to get you to agree with their bullshit, try this structure:

1. "When you..." (describe what they are doing that you want them to stop)

2. "I feel..." (describe exactly what sort of negative feeling is created)

3. "If you stopped..." (specify the objectionable behaviour)
   "and instead..." (describe the behaviour you want)

4. "Then I am going to feel..." (the feeling you want to have; a better outcome)[7]

GOOD HABITS
Practice a more inquisitive approach to become adept at countering bullshit.

- **BURST YOUR BUBBLE**: read more widely to experience different views
- **ENGAGE 'SYSTEM TWO'**: this is your more logical, considered response, not your emotional response
- **LEARN SOME STATS**: inform yourself on topics where you often encounter bullshit
- **TREAT NARRATIVES YOU BELIEVE AS SCEPTICALLY AS ONES YOU DON'T**: question your own views
- **TRY NOT TO SUCCUMB TO CONSPIRATORIAL THINKING**: it might be true, but it might not[9]

CHEEKY TACTICS: IF ALL ELSE FAILS...
- Take what they have just said literally and reveal the exaggerations and absurdities of it
- Translate it into plain and clear English, and say it back to them to show how ludicrous it all sounds
- Say: "You sound ridiculous. Do you want to retract that?"

II. REMOVING BULLSHIT FROM BUSINESS

MINIMIZE BULLSHIT PRODUCTION

According to André Spicer, in his book *Business Bullshit*, most organizations are flooded with empty talk, and it's killing them because 'management speak' has become more important than long-lasting results. Bullshit statements have one signature feature: they are unclarifiable – they are not only obscure, but they cannot be rendered *unobscure*.[17] The primary way to remove this obscurity is to minimize bullshit production. He suggests six ways to do it:

1. **ELIMINATE BULLSHIT JOBS**: many people feel they have jobs that are utterly meaningless, so review and remove these.

2. **CUT BACK ON CORPORATE ESCAPISM**: awayday preening exercises rarely result in action, so just set direction and ask people to get on with it.

3. **PROVIDE EMPLOYEES SOME SECURITY**: most bullshit is generated by people who are insecure in their jobs, so clarify the safety of these roles.

4. **GIVE EMPLOYEES SPACE TO ASK QUESTIONS**: that means not being scared to state that something appears to be bullshit, and then fixing it.

5. **FORGET BEST PRACTICE**: lots of initiatives are started just because the competition is doing it, but doing it your way is better.

6. **FOCUS ON STABILITY**: managerial bullshit is obsessed with change, and many organizations suffer from *repetitive change syndrome*. Define what you are good at and stick to it.[17]

SLOW DOWN BULLSHIT EXCHANGE

Bullshit exchange almost becomes a ritual in many companies – a way of life. Here are some ways to slow down the exchange of bullshit:

1. **REALITY TEST**: get the facts on whether something truly works or not, before initiating it.

2. **RATIONALITY TEST**: poor reasoning is a hallmark of bullshit. Always ask: why does this need to be done at all?

3. **MEANING TEST**: do the concepts genuinely make sense to the audience? If not, ditch the project or come up with something better and clearer.

4. **INTENTIONALITY TEST**: what intentions and motives lie behind the bullshit? Are we deluding ourselves here?

5. **CLARIFIABILITY TEST**: can this thing actually be clarified, and will it definitely help the business?[17]

STOP REWARDING BULLSHIT

Cultures that reward bullshit just get worse and worse. Here are six ways to stop rewarding bullshit:

1. **LIMIT ATTENTION TO IT**: do not publicize shoddy work.

2. **DON'T LEGITIMIZE IT**: don't endorse it or approve of it.

3. **PROVIDE ALTERNATIVE BASES OF SELF-CONFIDENCE**: promote clearer expression and communication.

4. **MAKE STUPIDITY COSTLY**: highlight examples of vague and obscure communication.

5. **MAKE INCREASING ORGANIZATIONAL LOAD COSTLY**: constantly try to remove layers of bullshit from the company.

6. **TRACK TRUST**: introduce a metric that links clear, non-bullshit communication with better understanding, trust and effective results.[17]

BE MORE DISTINCTIVE TO COMMUNICATE BETTER
Orwell recommended that whenever you're crafting a message, there are ways to make sure it is bullshit-free (my word, not his).[2] Scrupulous writers need to ask of every sentence:

1. **WHAT AM I TRYING TO SAY?** Clear intent from the start.

2. **WHAT WORDS WILL EXPRESS IT?** Think hard.

3. **WHAT IMAGE OR IDIOM WILL MAKE IT CLEARER?** Is there one?

4. **IS THIS IMAGE FRESH ENOUGH TO HAVE AN EFFECT?** If not, think of a better one.

5. **COULD I PUT IT MORE CONCISELY?** Ruthlessly self-edit.

6. **HAVE I SAID ANYTHING THAT IS AVOIDABLY UGLY?** If so, improve it.

Overall, always challenge yourself to find different ways to say things. Look for a wider vocabulary to convey thinking and communication that is fresh, novel, independent, individual, genuine, leading, unparalleled, incomparable, exclusive, rare, different, imaginative, inspired, and hopefully more special than that of others.

SPECIFICALLY WHEN WRITING...
Orwell recommends that you try to follow these rules:[2]

1. **NEVER USE A METAPHOR, SIMILE OR OTHER FIGURE OF SPEECH WHICH YOU ARE USED TO SEEING IN PRINT.** Doing so just makes you sound like everyone else.

2. **NEVER USE A LONG WORD WHERE A SHORT ONE WILL DO.** Brevity is everything.

3. **IF IT IS POSSIBLE TO CUT A WORD OUT, CUT IT OUT.** More ruthless self-editing.

4. **NEVER USE THE PASSIVE WHERE YOU CAN USE THE ACTIVE.** Action-based verbs work best.

5. **NEVER USE A FOREIGN PHRASE, A SCIENTIFIC WORD OR A JARGON WORD IF YOU CAN THINK OF AN EVERYDAY ENGLISH EQUIVALENT.** Exotic flair is vaguer than the precision of your own language.

6. **BREAK ANY OF THESE RULES SOONER THAN SAY ANYTHING OUTRIGHT BARBAROUS.**

WHEN WORKING WITH THE MEDIA

Pay attention to how you and your company interact with the media. Watch the headlines you wish to generate. Complexity is not a virtue. Try to be absolutely honest and objective about how you report information and events. Explain how you work, get out of the bubble, and help your audience do the same. If you want to be trusted, be trustworthy. Think about where you get your content. If your company or product has reputation issues, look at why parts of your audience are leaving.[9]

CLEAR COMMUNICATION APPROACHES

- **BOTTOM LINE UPFRONT** is the best way to start any presentation: your message is immediately clear and remains so even if the meeting or conversation is cut short or someone has to leave early.[19]
- **WIFM** stands for *What's In It For Me?* All presenters should consider this question in relation to the people they are presenting to. Know what motivates your audience, skip what doesn't matter, and make a conclusive delivery.
- **FLAGGING** is calling out the number of ideas you want to share. This provides an order to any presentation, and keeps the audience connected, waiting for you to deliver that number of points.
- **TLDR** stands for *Too Long, Didn't Read* and *TLDW* stands for *Too Long, Didn't Watch*. Make sure your material doesn't fall into these categories.

A CLASSIC ARGUMENT SHAPE

Don't simply declare what you believe – offer arguments. Arguments are not shouting matches; they are supposed to be constructive. An argument is defined as when someone (the arguer) presents one claim (the premise) as a reason of some kind for another claim (the conclusion).[18] It is a connected series of statements intended to present a reason for a proposition.

A classic argument shape is:

- **OBSERVATION**: "I see that..."
- **HYPOTHESIS**: "So, I think that 'x' is the case..."
- **COMPARISON**: "This explanation is better than other possibilities..."
- **CONCLUSION**: "Therefore, 'x' is the case..."

Use this as the basis of a bullshit-free conversation.

There are also many ways to be civil when arguing:

1. **RE-EXPRESS THE OTHER PERSON'S POSITION CLEARLY.** Do it vividly and fairly, so they wish they had put it that way themselves.

2. **LIST ANY POINTS OF AGREEMENT.** This provides the basis for common ground.

3. **MENTION ANYTHING THAT YOU HAVE LEARNED FROM THEM.** This flatters them and provides a basis on which to move the discussion forward.

4. **ONLY THEN ARE YOU PERMITTED TO CHALLENGE OR CRITICIZE.** *Argument markers* are words like 'so' and 'because' that signal that an argument is being given. They move things along. If at all possible, try to avoid *infinite regress*, which is when an argument never ends because there is always another level of justification needed.[18]

POINTING OUT BULLSHIT

In America, this is called *calling out bullshit* or *calling bullshit*. It is important that people do this, otherwise the bullshit just carries on and the perpetrators continue to get away with it. You don't have to be rude when you do this, and there are many ways to do it, many of them in this book. In essence:

* Check the facts to be as certain as you can that you are right
* Be gracious if you are not right
* Try to say something more distinctive than the bullshitter
* Look for other examples that provide an alternative to their view

BAN THE BULLSHIT AND TELL EVERYONE

There are over 50 ways in this section to reduce, or even completely remove, bullshit from business life. Railing against bullshit is a non-stop crusade. Those who are serious about it need to:

1. STOP USING BULLSHIT THEMSELVES.

2. POINT OUT WHEN OTHERS ARE USING IT.

3. LET EVERYONE KNOW THAT THIS IS A BULLSHIT-FREE CULTURE.

That means frowning on it in meetings, emails, conversations, and all marketing material such as brochures, publicity material and websites.

It is possible to be bullshit-free. You now have the knowledge and techniques. Over to you.

III. A MANIFESTO FOR A BULLSHIT-FREE WORLD

WHAT IS BULLSHIT?

- Bullshit mostly means deceptive misrepresentation, a lack of concern for the truth, and an indifference to how things really are
- It's like shoddy goods – a kind of bluff
- Bullshit is not just words; it's data, graphics, images and much more
- Bullshit is not lying. It's all the stuff in between truth and lies, although much of it is just short of lying
- In first-degree bullshit, the speaker knows they are bullshitting
- In second-degree bullshit, they may just be lazy or ignorant
- The relationship between the stance and the message matters
  Does the person really believe the words they are saying?
- Who is saying this? Can they be trusted? Do they have a history of talking bullshit?
- Bad thinking leads to bad expression, and bad expression leads to bad thinking
- There is no limit to bullshit — there is an infinite supply
- Remember that bullshit is harder to spot than you think, because it is neither on the side of the truth nor the false
- Given all these possible permutations, we should always treat information with great suspicion until we know the real story

WHY PEOPLE DO IT

- The seven main reasons why people bullshit are:

  1. To impress
  2. To persuade
  3. To cover up

4. To evade
5. To confuse
6. To manipulate
7. To mislead

- These are on an approximate sliding scale, from mild and relatively harmless to strong and dangerous

HOW DANGEROUS IS IT?

- Language matters, and the more bullshit is used, the more dangerous it becomes
- Bullshit language leads to bullshit thinking, and vice versa
- If everyone is talking the same bullshit, people and companies will suffer from the problem of sameness, with no one being distinctive
- Escalated to a higher level, bullshit has the power to devalue truth
- Company leaders and entire cultures can be undermined by bullshit
- Creating bullshit is easy and any fool can do it
- Clearing up after bullshit is often impossible and the price of trying to do so is often high, if only through the amount of work needed to refute it
- Sometimes, you are your own source of bullshit. It is your responsibility to examine this possibility very carefully

DEALING WITH BULLSHITTERS

- Cross-examine them with a range of penetrating questions
- Ask yourself several questions about what they have said
- Analyze carefully what they said
- Reason and argue with what they have said
- Question the numbers
- Explain your feelings on the subject, and how their bullshit makes you feel
- Develop good habits of your own to consider wider views
- If all else fails, resort to some cheeky tactics

REMOVING BULLSHIT FROM YOUR BUSINESS

- Minimize bullshit production
- Slow down bullshit exchange
- Stop rewarding bullshit
- Be more distinctive, to communicate better
- Work hard to be bullshit-free when writing and working with media
- Adopt clear communication approaches and a classic shape to arguments
- Point out bullshit whenever you see or hear it
- Ban the bullshit and tell everyone

IV. BIBLIOGRAPHY

A Field Guide To Lies And Statistics, Daniel Levitin (Penguin, 2016)

Afterliff: The New Dictionary Of Things There Should be A Word for, Lloyd & Canter (Faber & Faber, 2013)

A Word In Your Shell-Like, Nigel Rees (Harper Collins, 2006)

Bad Language, Graham Edmonds (Southbank, 2008)

Brief, Joseph McCormack (Wiley, 2014)

Brewer's Dictionary Of Phrase and Fable, Ivor Evans (Cassell, 1975)

Bullshit Bingo, Graham Edmonds (Southbank, 2005)

Bullshit Jobs, David Graeber (Allen Lane, 2018)

Business Bullshit, André Spicer (Routledge, 2018)

Calling Bullshit: The Art of Scepticism In A Data-Driven World, Bergstrom & West (Allen Lane, 2020)

Death Sentences, Don Watson (Gotham, 2005)

Ducks In A Row: An A-Z of Offlish, Carl Newbrook (Short Books, 2005)

English Dictionary (Collins, 2003)

How To Be Right, James O'Brien (Penguin, 2018)

How To Make The World Add Up, Tim Harford (The Bridge Street Press, 2021)

Leadership BS, Jeffrey Pfeffer (Harper Business, 2015)

Liar's Paradise, Graham Edmonds (Southbank, 2006)

Never Split The Difference, Chris Voss (Random House, 2016)

No Bullshit Leadership, Chris Hirst (Profile Books, 2019)

Non-Bullshit Innovation, David Rowan (Transworld Publishers, 2019)

On Bullshit, Harry G Frankfurt (Princeton University Press, 2005)

Oxford Dictionary of Humorous Quotations, Gyles Brandreth (Oxford, 2015)

Politics And The English Language, George Orwell (Penguin 2013)

Post Truth, Matthew D'Ancona (Ebury Press, 2017)

Post-Truth: How Bullshit Conquered The World, James Ball (Biteback, 2017)

Red Herrings And White Elephants, Albert Jack (Metro Publishing, 2004)

Spin-glish, Beard & Cerf (Blue Rider Press, 2015)

Surrounded By Psychopaths, Thomas Erikson (Vermilion, 2017)

The Business Bullshit Book, Kevin Duncan (LID Business Media, 2016)

The Complete Uxbridge English Dictionary, Garden & Naismith (Penguin Random House, 2016)

The Completely Superior Person's Book of Words, Peter Bowler (Bloomsbury, 2009)

The Dictionary of Business Bullshit, Kevin Duncan (LID Business Media, 2013)

The Dictionary of Business Nonsense, Kevin Duncan (Viva, 2017)

The Intelligence Trap, David Robson (Hodder, 2019)

The Language Wars, Henry Hitchings (John Murray, 2011)

The Life-Changing Science of Detecting Bullshit, John V Petrocelli (St Martin's Press, 2021)

The Meaning of Liff, Adams & Lloyd (Pan Books, 1983)

The New Collins Thesaurus (Collins, 1987)

The Prevalence of Humbug, Max Black (Cornell University Press, 1983)

Think Again: How To Reason And Argue, Walter Sinnott-Armstrong (Pelican, 2018)

Through The Language Glass, Guy Deutscher (Arrow, 2011)

Who Touched Base In My Thought Shower?, Steven Poole (Sceptre, 2014)

Why Business People Speak Like Idiots, Fugere, Hardaway & Warshawsky (Free Press, 2005)

V. **REFERENCES**

1. *The Language Wars*, Henry Hitchings (John Murray, 2011)

2. *Politics And The English Language*, George Orwell (Penguin 2013)

3. *The Prevalence of Humbug*, Max Black (Cornell University Press, 1983)

4. *On Bullshit*, Harry G Frankfurt (Princeton University Press, 2005)

5. *Calling Bullshit: The Art of Scepticism In A Data-Driven World*, Bergstrom & West (Allen Lane, 2020)

6. "Garry Kasparov," Goodreads, last accessed August 5, 2021, https://www.goodreads.com/quotes/8220792-the-point-of-modern-propaganda-isn-t-only-to-misinform-or

7. *Surrounded By Psychopaths*, Thomas Erikson (Vermilion, 2017)

8. "George Carlin," Goodreads, last accessed August 5, 2021, https://www.goodreads.com/quotes/25610-honesty-may-be-the-best-policy-but-it-s-important-to

9. *Post-Truth: How Bullshit Conquered The World*, James Ball (Biteback, 2017)

10. *No Bullshit Leadership*, Chris Hirst (Profile Books, 2019)

11. *Leadership BS*, Jeffrey Pfeffer (Harper Business, 2015)

12 *The War For Talent*, Michaels & Handfield-Jones (Harvard Business Review Press, 2001)

13. Peter Cook, "A Brief History of Thought Leadership," Peter Cook, August 15, 2012, https://petercook.com/blog/a-brief-history-of-thought-leadership

14. *Scarne On Cards*, John Scarne (Signet, 1991)

15. "Origins of the phrase 24/7," Reddit, last accessed August 5, 2021, https://www.reddit.com/r/etymology/comments/hhccxo/origins_of_the_phrase_247

16. *The Legacy of Hiroshima*, Edward Teller (Praeger, 1975)

17. *Business Bullshit*, André Spicer (Routledge, 2018)

18. *Think Again: How To Reason And Argue*, Walter Sinnott-Armstrong (Pelican, 2018)

19. *Brief*, Joseph McCormack (Wiley, 2014)

VI. RESOURCES

Head to bulldictionary.com for general amusement and regular updates.

Head to greatesthitsblog.com for one-page summaries of 500 business books.

Watch 'Why BS is more dangerous than a lie,' a 13-minute TedX talk by John V. Petrocelli. https://www.youtube.com/watch?v=WaOiRRqHNNk

ABOUT THE AUTHOR

KEVIN DUNCAN is a business adviser, marketing expert, motivational speaker and author. After 20 years in advertising and direct marketing, he has spent the last 20 years as an independent troubleshooter, advising companies on how to change their businesses for the better.

CONTACT THE AUTHOR FOR ADVICE, TRAINING OR SPEAKING OPPORTUNITIES:

kevinduncanexpertadvice@gmail.com
@kevinduncan
expertadviceonline.com
bulldictionary.com

ALSO BY THE AUTHOR:

- *Business Greatest Hits*
- *How to Run and Grow Your Own Business*
- *How To Tame Technology And Get Your Life Back*
- *Marketing Greatest Hits*
- *Marketing Greatest Hits Vol.2*
- *Revolution*
- *Run Your Own Business*
- *Small Business Survival*
- *So What?*
- *Start*
- *Start Your Own Business*
- *The Business Bullshit Book*
- *The Diagrams Book*
- *The Excellence Book*
- *The Ideas Book*
- *The Intelligent Work Book*
- *The Smart Strategy Book*
- *The Smart Thinking Book*
- *Tick Achieve*
- *What You Need to Know About Starting A Business*

BOOK SUMMARY

Bullshit is everywhere. Some of it is just lazy and some is complete nonsense, yet some is at least trying to communicate something, even if it fails. After 40 years of railing against vague language and bull, best-selling author Kevin Duncan is uniquely qualified to comment on why and where it all happens. Whilst we may never eradicate it, Kevin is on a mission to improve business language and understanding.

His laser-sharp inquisitiveness weeds out the worst offenders and the contexts in which they most frequently occur. He defines their attempted meaning, looks at their use and abuse and gives us intelligent ways to better articulate the sentiments they are trying to express – in plain English. Its companion guide *The Business Bullshit Book* contains over 2,000 examples and definitions to provide a complete body of work.